"This is a powerful book ... guilt and fear you have ... for your kids. Then it wil... ... at the opportunity everywhere for kids to gain confidence and mastery, if we have the courage to get out of the way and let them."
— Isaac Morehouse, Founder & CEO of Praxis

"Teri's book is well researched and includes great information about the Charlotte Mason teaching philosophy, which the Apologia curricula encourage. The motto of Charlotte Mason's organization was 'Education is an atmosphere, a discipline, and a life.' Similarly, homeschooling is often referred to as a lifestyle where children should be allowed to dive deep into an area of study. As they explore creation outside, rather than sitting for long hours at an uncomfortable desk set in the confines of a windowless room, they will energetically discover the wonders of God's amazing handiwork. Narrating, writing, and drawing their observations in notebooking journals are great ways for this to happen. Being in the context of a loving family combined with a natural processing of the world around them develops high retention of the information and a life-long love of learning without the stress that can come from long hours of work on subjects that they don't find interesting."
— Davis Carman, president of Apologia Educational Ministries

DYING TO WIN

HOW TO INSPIRE AND IGNITE YOUR CHILD'S LOVE OF LEARNING IN AN OVERSTRESSED WORLD

TERI CAPSHAW

Printed in the United States of America

Published by Author Academy Elite
P.O. Box 43, Powell, OH 43035
www.AuthorAcademyElite.com

Paperback ISBN-13: 978-1-64085-152-8
Hardcover ISBN-13: 978-1-64085-153-5
Library of Congress Control Number: 2017914899

Cover Design: Veerle Vermillion

For DeAnna Fay.
My first teacher — and my mom.
Thank you for making learning an adventure every day.

And for my husband, Jesse.
I couldn't have done it without your support and
encouragement.

TABLE OF CONTENTS

PART 2 IGNITE A PASSION FOR LIFE: 7 STEPS TO INSPIRE YOUR CHILD

PART 3 BREAKING FREE: BUILD AN EDUCATIONAL FAMILY LEGACY

FOREWORD

We all understand that schools are failing our students. After nine overhauls of our public education system in twenty-seven years, and a continual degradation in our educational standing in the world, who would argue that it's not still broken? What's more disturbing is that even when we know they're failing we, as parents, have been programmed to send our kids to school anyway.

When I wrote *They're YOUR Kids*, I opened the book with a startling quotation from a man who influenced the entire public school movement:

> *"Education should aim at destroying free will so that after pupils are thus schooled they will be incapable throughout the rest of their lives of thinking or acting otherwise than as their schoolmasters would have wished ... When the technique has been perfected, every government that has been in charge of education for more than one generation will be able to control its subjects securely without the need of armies or policemen."*

That approach was advocated by Johann Gottliebe Fichte — the head of philosophy and psychology at the Prussian University in Berlin. More than a century after his death British philosopher Bertrand Russell would quote Fichte in *The Impact of Science On Society*.

In the same book, which was published in 1952, Russell made this claim:

> *"The social psychologists of the future will have a number of classes of school children on whom they will try different methods of producing an unshakable conviction that snow is black. Various results will soon be arrived at. First, that the influence of home is obstructive. Second, that not much can be done unless the indoctrination begins before the age of ten. Third, that verses set to music and repeatedly intoned are very effective. Fourth, that the opinion that snow is white must be held to show a morbid taste for eccentricity. But I anticipate. It is for future scientists to make these maxims precise and discover how much it costs per head to make children believe that snow is black and how much less it would cost to make them believe that it is dark gray."*

Today our schools are teaching an even greater lie: our children are told that they are accidents of nature and that "survival of the fittest" is the law of the land.

It seems Russell's perspective is winning out as our historically Judeo-Christian culture, built upon morals and values, slowly crumbles, taking with it the values of life, liberty, and private property.

When our children are taught from a "survival of the fittest" mindset is it any surprise that bullying is out of control in our schools? That siblings can't get along? Or that teenage rebellion is viewed as normal? Or, as this book explores, that the pressure to be the "best" is a global problem driving some students to the brink of suicide?

It has never been more important for parents to be empowered to take charge of their children's education. Teachers can be really wonderful and pour into children's lives in meaningful ways. But the education system itself has been corrupted and parents need to be informed that they are not superfluous, but necessary for the proper education of their children.

A lot of parents feel inadequate to the task of educating their youngsters because they were taught in school that unless they were specifically instructed in how to do something, they were incapable of doing it. Hogwash!

I had my own share of doubts when I started homeschooling my three children. This is partly why I wrote *They're YOUR Kids;* to empower parents in this daunting process. There are so many options available now, online and in community, to home educate. Over the years I have not only found the right resources and approach to meet my children's needs, I have learned so much from others who have chosen a similar path.

But the benefits don't stop there. By the time you are reading this, "Let There Be Light," a feature film I co-wrote, produced and co-star in, will be released in theaters nationwide. It's one of my many projects that simply wouldn't have happened outside of our family choosing to homeschool. It wasn't just the added flexibility that home schooling gave me with my schedule, it was the confidence and understanding that we all can be life-long learners, capable innovators, that I learned by embracing the task of becoming my children's "lead-learner."

While incredibly educational, sharing so much of life with my children has even greater value from the standpoint of the relationships we're developing with each other and in the world. Far from being institutionalized each day, my children engage the world, doing speech and debate competitions, working and volunteering, even speaking publicly at school board meetings. The result of children of different ages sharing their days together means they get along better than they did when my oldest was in school, lording his superiority, based solely on his age, over his younger siblings. My personal relationships with each child is necessarily deeper than if I saw them for only two hours or moments each day. My children are an intense and appreciated blessing to both my husband and me.

That's why I feel called to empower parents to explore fully the blessings your children can introduce in your lives! You are about to find out that you *are* more capable than you ever imagined — and that there are plenty of resources available to help you take charge of your children's education.

Most importantly, I want you to know that God gave you your children for a reason. It wasn't by chance or luck of the draw. And if you choose to send that gift away everyday instead of opening it up and discovering what's inside, then you're missing something precious and specifically intended for you.

Sam Sorbo
Author of *They're YOUR Kids: An Inspirational Journey from Self-Doubter to Homeschool Advocate* and *Teach From Love: A School Year Devotional for Families*

INTRODUCTION

"Gor-don-dela Ribe-ye, Flame Grilled New York Strip, Herb Roasted Chicken…" Just over two weeks away from her fifth birthday my daughter stumbled reading the words on a Gordon Biersch take-out menu. My husband laughed with her over the mistakes and congratulated her on the lines she pronounced correctly. (If you're curious, the first was Gorgonzola Ribeye. And now you're hungry. Sorry.)

The appetite she has for learning — and challenging herself to improve in reading and many other areas — reminds me of why I felt compelled to write this book. Whether she's sneaking a peek at my cell phone text messages or expertly setting her little brother up for a nap with "just the right amount of story to make him sleepy" — reading has become a part of her identity.

Friends and family speculate as to whether she's naturally talented or merely driven to succeed. My husband and I often discuss our suspicions that most children can do far more than they or their parents realize. But really, we don't know. What we do know is that our daughter is getting an opportunity to learn all she wants in a low-stress way that suits her personality.

Our goal is not for our children to merely meet certain milestones early. Instead, we want to give each of our children a "red-tape free" education. We want to create an appetite — a true hunger — for learning. Rather than push them into things they are not yet ready to learn, we are careful to make sure we don't limit what we *allow* them to learn based on cultural expectations.

In this book I want to help you look at your children's education in a new way. But I know it's not easy to shake the feeling that you're failing your child if you don't follow a familiar process. I feel the same pressure to make sure my kids are hitting specific milestones by certain ages — and the expectation that I'll provide a "normal" childhood for my children by enrolling them in a traditional school.

So what does that have to do with looking at what's happening in schools on the other side of the globe? Well, we're living in a world more interconnected than ever before. In fact, for the past century the United States has projected so much influence that it is often said, "when America sneezes, the world catches a cold." But this time, America is feeling the chill.

By dominating standardized tests, China sends a powerful message about its rising status with potential to eclipse the world's biggest economy. And it's working. Wealthy American parents are scrambling to secure native Mandarin speaking nannies for their children. Almost everyone asks why our kids can't compete on tests. And I bought my daughter Singapore Early Bird Kindergarten math. When she was three.

Chinese education is wildly successful, dangerous, and contagious. In fact, many people in the US who tacitly support homeschooling do so only because testing shows, on average, students in US public schools are underperforming compared to those in other developed nations. Homeschooling is often viewed as "Plan B" in a world where schools aren't accomplishing what people expect.

As someone who was educated at home from kindergarten through high school graduation I always accepted that perspective as reasonable — until a big move sent my family to Taiwan. Suddenly I was in a part of the world where students tend to ace international tests. I soon realized the educational experience many students are getting in Asia falls far short of what you and I want for our own children. Indeed, many parents there are just as concerned about problems with public education in their own countries as US parents are about weaknesses in our system.

Because I know that you want the best for your children I want you to fully understand what's going on in education systems in these economically powerful countries. I will also take a deep dive into how public policy may be pushing American schools in the same direction. Then, I'm going to look at the economic incentives in place for companies to keep profiting from pushing more and more hours of school and tutoring on kids everywhere — regardless of the results.

It's not always fun or easy to tell friends and family that you want to take a different approach to life, but you owe it to your children to consider carefully what academic success really looks like. There is a better approach — a new "Plan A."

PART 1

DYING TO WIN: WHEN WINNING CAUSES THE GREATEST LOSS

THE PAINFUL SIDE EFFECTS
OF VICTORY

*"Our schools produce exceptional results,
but the burdens are severe."*

*Wang Jianjun
Professor at East China Normal*[1]

Abright ten-year-old jumped from the fifth floor of her apartment building after performing poorly on her midterm tests. According to newspaper reports the Singapore girl was generally cheerful and had a supportive father who showed up for her school events. However, two weeks before committing suicide Lysher Loh told the family maid that she didn't want to be reincarnated as a person because she would have to do homework, go to school, and fight with siblings.[2]

The story made headlines in 2001 as the city-state's "Thinking Schools, Learning Nation" initiative was well underway.[3] Yet somehow the young girl took her work more seriously than anyone intended. According to the coroner, "She had been advised by her teachers to be less meticulous so as not to give herself added stress."

A decade later, 10-year-old Ethan Ng made a final entry in his journal, "I want to die, I want to kill myself. I want to be put into jail. I want death." The Hong Kong boy then jumped from his fifth-floor apartment. According to a news report, a month earlier he "failed his Chinese examination and was duly 'reproached' by his parents. His music teacher also criticized him for his poor performance." He was one of five Hong Kong students ages 10 to 16 to commit suicide in November 2011.[4]

In China, a 13-year-old boy hanged himself in April 2014. The apparent trigger was unfinished homework.[5]

In the Hebei province, balconies surround the Hengshui No. 2 secondary school's open-air courtyard.[6] Students probably already feel trapped in the rigorous institution where the wake-up call reportedly comes at 5:30 a.m. and students study until 10:10 p.m. They have three 40-minute meal breaks.[7]

Now the many floors of balconies feature what look something like jail bars running to the ceiling. The "anti-suicide" barriers make the halls resemble a sort of long cage. Red banners on the outside of the bars encourage students to "study hard." The institution is known as one of the top 100 schools in China. By April 2015, two of the school's students had already committed suicide ahead of the all-important "Gaokao" exam.

Passing the Gaokao exam is the only way for students in China to get into a university.[8] Ensuring a young student makes the cut for college admission becomes an obsession in many Chinese families. These days many people there, like many Americans, want their children to get college degrees since most better paying jobs require one. And in many families, children are under pressure to do well financially so they can care for their parents in old age. In China, the government's one-child policy has created a situation where the weight of that burden is placed on the only child a couple was allowed to have. As a result, competition is fierce.

The intense effort to help students cram information into their heads is almost unbelievable. In 2012, pictures circulated in international news reports showing IV bags for students rigged up in a classroom. Apparently, the teachers set up the bags just to be helpful. The teens and their parents seemed to think that taking amino acids for energy this way is a common sense approach as they study for the Gaokao.[9]

It's logical to assume that widespread intense preparation affects the mental health of students. And the numbers are alarming. About 24% of Shanghai students have thought about committing suicide, 15% seriously considered it, and more than 5% actually planned it. Another 1.7% attempted to commit suicide in the past.

In 2014, the Chinese Communist party estimated that about 500 students commit suicide each year. It seems that 2/3 of those students take their lives during the second semester of the school year — when they face high-stakes exams. A government document blames most suicides on the students' inability to, "handle the immense pressure caused by the examination-based education system."[5]

Ironically, perhaps the worst part of this tragedy is that changing the Chinese educational system may be nearly impossible due to its incredible success. Asian countries are among the current standard bearers for educational achievement worldwide.

Students in Shanghai, Singapore, and Hong Kong claim the top three spots in the 2012 Programme for International Student Assessment (PISA).[10] Shanghai students scored a full three years ahead of the world's average student. But what caught the eye of the world is the vast difference between China's students, who came out on top, and American students who ranked 27 out of 34 countries.

This may prompt American parents to think they should emulate China's educational approach. However, in China some parents, teachers, and administrators realize there has to be more to education that what they are seeing. Their best must somehow be better.

Ironically, at a time when China struggles to shake the worst parts of its education system, the United States has been implementing a national program to emulate it — in a system that apparently already has students dying to fit in.

MYOPIA

Some children in Yangiang, China spend their days in what is essentially a glass classroom. Translucent walls allow sunshine to fill the entire space. Why? A full 80% of Beijing teenagers are nearsighted. Studies have shown that spending time outdoors seems to help prevent Myopia. School officials hope to bring the benefits of being outdoors into the classroom even as students continue to study.[11]

CHAPTER REVIEW

Based on raw academic test scores, Asian countries regularly rank among the best in the world, but their students are paying a high price for the honor. American parents should consider the consequences carefully before taking a similar approach.

PRE-EXISTING CONDITIONS

*"Every successful florist well understands that the outside
conditions and influences that cause one plant or flower to
develop and bloom dwarfs, stunts, and even crushes others of
a different class. Knowing this shall we not begin at once a
thorough study of child-nature?"*

Lida Brooks Miller, *The Kindergarten* (1894)

My husband and I were out enjoying a beautiful
Saturday afternoon. Although we did struggle a
bit to navigate strollers over rough chunks of sidewalk, through a Japanese restaurant's outdoor seating, and
around Taichung's ubiquitous scooters. Finally, we saw relief:
a sidewalk, wide enough to serve as a road, which skirts one
of the city's fenced school grounds. Suddenly a gate opened
and hundreds of uniformed high school students filled every
available space.

We realized then that we were the only people nearby even
trying to enjoy a day off. We were, as a Taiwanese friend of
mine would describe it, living on "American time."

There's certainly something to be said for knowing how
to relax. But at a time when Taiwan assembles 90% of the

world's laptops and 98% of all computer motherboards, a case can also be made for taking notes.[12] Exactly what are our counterparts in Asia doing right to attract so much business while America's manufacturing industry languishes?

The latest public school reform effort that swept America attempts to respond with a new set of standards — assuming that higher standards will prompt students to achieve more and become internationally competitive. According to the Common Core State Standards website, "standards from top-performing countries played a significant role in the development of the math and English language arts/literacy standards."[13] And on the all-important topic of math education, the organization points out that, "the progression in the Common Core State Standards is mathematically coherent and leads to college and career readiness at an internationally competitive level." This claim seems to line up with observations made in a document released by the administrators of a major international test. A document released by the Organisation for Economic Co-operation and Development says that Common Core Mathematics Standards appear to be "influenced substantially by PISA itself."[14]

There is a complex raging debate over whether these new standards will really deliver on that promise — especially whether they are indeed "mathematically coherent." But an even more important question is left unasked. What if it actually works? What if American students are somehow successfully ushered into this ultra-competitive academic sphere?

Calling on our children to strive for excellence is a worthy endeavor, but we need to keep in mind that students in top performing countries aren't just scoring higher because they're working smarter. They are sacrificing huge amounts of time — and their families are spending a large portion of their incomes to make sure they ace those tests. (We'll take a look at the incredible economic cost of academic success in the next chapter.)

Most importantly, we need to consider pre-existing conditions in the American education system that just might make our children even more susceptible to problems. It takes little time outside of the United States to realize that individualism is the primary characteristic of American culture. And like any culture, it has strengths and weaknesses. It's unlikely you'll find scores of American high school students studying 14 hours a day. However, they have their own share of troubles — the sources of which are far more difficult to determine.

One study found that for American high school students, the suicide rate actually decreases when school is out of session. In their paper, entitled "Back to School Blues: Seasonality of youth suicide and the academic calendar," researchers Benjamin Hansen and Matthew Lang set out to determine why the "suicide rate of 15-19 year olds tripled between 1950 and 1990" even as the rates for older people dropped.[15]

In a study they believe to be the first of its kind, they looked at the relationship between school and youth suicide. They found that "during months that students tend to be on break from school (June, July, August, and December), youth suicide is significantly lower than the rest of the year."

While the exact cause for this pattern is difficult to determine, the researchers did notice the effect of education policies aimed at helping kids get ahead by spending more time in school. They observed, "The results above not only show a distinct drop in suicide during the summer months, coinciding with a break from the stress of secondary school, but may help explain the recent rise in youth suicide over the past half century as the length of the school year increases and academic standards rise."

In his book, *The Hurried Child*, psychologist Dr. David Elkind makes a strong argument for taking cultural tendencies into consideration when we try to make our kids more competitive:

"Our problems in American education arise because we are not sufficiently American, not because we are insufficiently British or Japanese. Our classrooms are not as individualized, and our curriculums are not as flexible, as our values of individualism and self-reliance demand. True educational reform will only come about when we make our education truly democratic, appropriate to children's individual growth rates and levels of mental development."[16]

University of Arkansas Professor Sandra Stotsky is a Common Core Standards validation committee member-turned-critic. She argues that an education system with greater state and local control is a valuable part of America's heritage, saying that the United States, "was the first country that was really based on that premise. That people were capable of governing themselves. They didn't need a monarch, they didn't need a dictator, they didn't need central planners. It's a huge and powerful idea — and we've almost lost sight of it."[17]

So how do we balance an inherited individualistic drive, our unique strength, with a practical desire to compete with the rest of the world? In the coming chapters, we'll meet a number of families who have answered that question in unique and creative ways — and achieved phenomenal results. But first we'll take a look at the billions of dollars on the line when students around the world face high-stakes exams.

CHAPTER REVIEW

Many American students already struggle with their own sources of anxiety. Adding on the burdens carried by their peers around the world isn't likely to help.

AMBITION AND OPPORTUNITY

"I think it's a natural human instinct, brought to excess by the anxious times we live in, that just wants my daughter to be the winner, even when I know winning is beside the point."

Anya Kamenetz,
The Test: Why Our Schools are Obsessed With Standardized Testing — But You Don't Have to Be

As a "rock-star teacher," Kim Ki-hoon earns $4 million (USD) a year. And, as he told a Wall Street Journal reporter, "The harder I work, the more I make."[18] He's a top hagwon ("cram school") teacher in South Korea, taking a sliver of the 78 billion dollar global tutoring market pie.

That dollar amount is projected to grow to more than $102.8 billion by 2018. According to market research firm Global Industry Analysts, $13.9 billion (about 15%) of that will be spent by parents in South Korea alone.[19]

These "shadow" education systems are called "hagwons" in South Korea, "juku" in Japan, "buke" in China, "tuition centers" in Singapore, "buxiban" in Taiwan, and "tutorial schools" in Hong Kong.

The Chinese spend the largest share of household income on education — a full 30%.[20] And what are they getting in return? A shot at a higher status — for many, a chance to enter the middle class. But these days the payoff isn't as impressive as the investment might suggest. In the last decade, an increase in graduates has caused the wage gap between college degree holders and migrant workers to shrink. One study showed that between 2003 and 2010 college graduates consistently made 1,500 yuan per month. Over the same period, monthly pay for migrant workers increased from 700 to 1200 yuan per month — a difference that amounts to less than the average amount families spend on education.[21] Worse yet, about a third of 2008 college graduates were unable to find work at all in their first year out of college.

Young graduates in Taiwan are also finding their degrees less relevant than expected. In the period from 2005 to 2010, only a quarter of all graduates found a job in their field of study. Of course, the really bad news has to do with unemployment numbers. The unemployment rate is not only increasing for graduates (from 2.7% to 5.84% over a 19-year period), but is actually higher for college graduates than those without a degree.[22]

In typical Taiwanese entrepreneurial style, Sung Keng-Lang, serves up chicken filets along with his opinions about degree depreciation in the modern economy. A couple of years into his doctoral program he dropped out of school to become a successful street vendor known as "Dr. Chicken." Now he warns students to think carefully about why they want to continue their educations and for those who have attained a high level of education to be willing to consider other opportunities, "Who says someone with a PhD cannot sell chicken?"[23]

Being flexible might just be the best advice for today. We live in a rapidly changing world where deciding how to prepare our children for their future careers is done imperfectly using snapshots of data — and hoping that the recent past has something to do with the future.

Despite having a population more than six times larger than South Korea, parents in the United States only spent about $5 billion on tutoring in 2012 compared to the $17 billion spent by parents in South Korea. But according to Washington Post Education Writer Valerie Strauss efforts to help America's kids become more competitive will fuel education spending, "If there's one common pattern in this era of corporate-influenced school reform: Whenever a new reform is introduced, new ways to make money off it inevitably follow."[24]

Tutoring and educational supply companies are certainly using the tag line "common-core aligned" as a marketing strategy, but in the US, the most significant factor is government money spent on education. Despite lagging behind in international achievement tests, the US does lead in one area globally: the amount of money spent on public education.[25] And it appears efforts to catch up academically will result in even more spending. In March 2015, CNBC reported that some of the biggest US education companies had already landed contracts worth hundreds of millions of dollars to help implement the Common Core Standards — and "despite some legal challenges and boycotts, more contracts potentially worth billions of dollars for testing, instructional materials and teacher training are on the way."[26]

This brings up two important questions:

1) Is the US actually on-track to duplicate Asia's success?
2) Is Asia's success worth duplicating?

When I first moved to Taiwan I was excited to learn as much as possible about teaching math. I thought if I asked around I could uncover some incredible strategies to help demystify the discipline for my children. What I really found was entire districts in my new home city seemingly primarily committed to tutoring.

I did read some information about various teaching techniques. After getting a few chapters into one book I spent more time than I should have agonizing over whether I would warp my daughter's development if I told her to "borrow a number" to complete addition or subtraction problems.

My engineer husband (who is sometimes called on to solved algebra problems during job interviews) finally settled the matter. He pointed out that the details don't matter when kids still spend countless hours drilling with tutors in order to excel. Perhaps the biggest difference between many kids in the US and most in Asia is the level of commitment on the part of parents willing to spend a large portion of their income — and hours of their children's time — on tutoring.

Sadly, those making huge sacrifices of time and money aren't getting the return they may expect. At a certain point learning the same thing as everyone else in the region doesn't offer a good return on investment. As a friend of mine put it, it's like a factory that's producing a huge quantity of one product: it doesn't matter how good the product is — at a certain point there's simply no more demand.

After experiencing life in Asia first-hand I now see the future for American kids not in competing with their peers around the world, but rather finding creative ways to complement what the world already has to offer. Our kids can and need to do better academically — and they will succeed when we inspire them to grasp the best attributes of American ingenuity. In the next section, we'll meet a number of parents who are giving their children the opportunity to do that — and ways you can set your child up for success as well.

SATURDAY SCHOOL IN AMERICA

It's far from Asia, but kids from more than 300 families in New Haven, Connecticut now attend classes on Saturday. From 8:00 a.m. until noon their public school teachers provide classes focused on math and reading — with some fun and games built into the program.[27]

Meanwhile, in Texas, Dallas Independent School District Trustee Miguel Solis believes a mandatory 20-minute recess will help boost kids' ability to learn.[28]

How to manage students' time is becoming an increasingly difficult feat as efforts to measure student and teacher performance has resulted in more time spent taking standardized exams. A study of 66 United States school districts shows that eighth graders spend the most time taking standardized tests: 25.3 hours per year. But even pre-K classes are affected, taking about four standardized tests each year.[12]

Boston Public Schools require second grade teacher Jeffrey Cipriani to administer three standardized tests each year. At that grade level, he says it takes about three weeks to administer the tests. He told the Washington Post, "It's a colossal amount of time." Adding that, "I probably spend about 60 hours not teaching reading but just sort of giving those assessments. They're valuable but not that valuable."[29]

PROFILE
Pam Morton: Test Stress in the Village

Academic anxiety isn't limited to countries with dominating economies. Working in a Nubian village in Egypt Pam Morton says parents are spending all they can to supplement their children's educations, "If you can afford anything at all your child will be tutored from the very start." She says, "And it may be three or four different kinds of tutors after school."

As in much of Asia, formal education often starts early in the small Nubian village — and the hours are long. As soon as they turn two, children are often enrolled in a French or English speaking school.

Through the Educan Development Corporation, Pam and her husband, John, go into villages where they help train teachers in classroom development, lesson planning, and professionalism.

She says parents in these rural areas have the same goals as parents everywhere: do the best they possibly can for their kids. But they're functioning in a flawed system since teachers are paid poorly and make money by picking up tutoring jobs after school, "So if the teacher in third grade doesn't meet her goal of teaching her lessons in the class it actually doesn't hurt because then she picks up tutoring students that she can teach on the side and earn extra money so it's a bit of a difficult situation because she doesn't necessarily want to fix the scenario."

Another challenge is dealing with a system that depends heavily on rote memorization where "It's all about the product and not the process." Pam says, "So the product is a perfect test, but the process to get there is not encouraged. Curiosity is not encouraged. It's just, 'Memorize the answer.'"

As a result, it's common for parents with students in preschool through 12th grade to borrow books used in the classroom so they can photocopy the information and rehearse it nightly in order to ace the year-end test. Pam says, "It's a very difficult system. If there's any variation in the learning or in the potential answer they just don't know what to do."

The Mortons recently had an opportunity to challenge local assumptions about education when they ran a pilot program introducing activity-based learning. The class of 15 preschool children met for 3 hours twice a week.

Pam says, "Everything was learning centers and fun and play and introducing Play Doh and scissors and all that kind of stuff — so that was totally on its ear from anything they've ever seen."

After three months, parents started seeing results. Some kids were more verbal and able to complete patterns. Teachers were encouraged to see their students suddenly doing things they weren't able to do before. As a result, Educan was invited to train more teachers to launch preschools. When the pilot project wrapped up Pam says some of the Egyptian ladies helping said, "We were not believers — we just thought this was crazy talk."

But in an educational culture where the only results that matter can be measured objectively, accepting a more relaxed approach even to preschool is a challenge.

"They kept saying when do they get their grade cards or when do they get their reports?" Pam says, "Because they just couldn't measure activity based learning. They were freaking out." Even when student progress was apparent, parents really wanted to know if their children got an "A." In the end they managed to create a list of 25 goals instead of more common benchmarking standards in an effort to convince parents that their kids were learning what they needed to learn without being graded.

One of the Mortons' goals is to help parents connect with their children more. Pam says parents are used to telling their children to do things, but sitting down for a conversation is a foreign concept. One mother said, "You mean my child wants me to talk to him?"

The preschool pilot program used materials easily accessible in the village so parents would believe that they could actually teach their children without the help of expensive imported educational props. In a place where it's common for parents to labor over architectural quality diorama structures to turn in for their children's preschool homework, the Mortons hope to redirect the investment of time and attention to helping children develop critical thinking skills through daily activities.

This challenge to focus on the child's development rather than on a completed product is nothing new to the Mortons, who have a background in various education settings in the region. At an international school, Pam says one student's mother epitomized one of the biggest problems when she was quick to come to her son's defense, "Don't blame him." She said when her son failed to turn in a homework assignment on time, "It was the maid's job to do it and it was the grandmother's job to put it in the backpack."

Sadly this relatively new global obsession with grades not only replaces authentic learning and growth — it may also be cheating children out of their cultural heritages. Pam says there's a price paid for investing everything into rehearsing a few academic subjects perfectly to the exclusion of anything else.

Older people notice that the kids don't learn how to weave, cook culturally unique foods, or make chairs out of bamboo trees. They also don't learn how to tell when local fruits, such a mango and dates, are ripe.

Ultimately, Pam says, "They're losing part of their heritage and their history because they aren't around to study it." After all, she says, "That part of their history won't get them into a college and it won't get them a scholarship so why would they be learning that right now?" Pam hopes to answer that question by showing the intrinsic value of cultivating a society of inquisitive, curious thinkers, "We're trying to chip away at it here." But she's afraid they'll make little progress without having the government adopt an entirely different approach to education.

In another part of the region, the Mortons found that modern global academic pressure combines with historical collective memory for a demoralizing effect.

At a training in Zanzibar, one of the headmasters said, "Oh, don't you know Zanzibar is the island of stupid, short, and ugly people?" Pam was shocked, "I was like 'What?' I mean this is one of their own." He said, "'Yeah, we're stupid, short, and ugly people.'" When Pam demanded to know why he would make such a claim the man explained that Zanzibar, an island off of Tanzania, was a slave trade port.

According to local lore, the only people who weren't sold and exported were short, ugly, and stupid. "So, he said, 'That's our gene pool. That's what we have to work with so we do what we can but that's what we've got.'"

Pam quickly realized that education there not only involves universal challenges, but also overcoming, "A long deep wound from way back about what they consider their capabilities are." An outlook on life inflicting pain for more than a century.

Living and working abroad in Egypt, Sudan, Kenya, and Tanzania has given Pam an appreciation for her own comfort ushering her own kids through their preschool years in America. When she sent her daughters to kindergarten, she remembers being asked if she stayed home with her kids. The teachers told her that they could tell because her daughters were farther along in their development due to the extra attention they got at home.

She tries to share that concept with the mothers she works with around the world but says the process won't work unless the moms know what to do with their kids when they do have them at home.

Over the years, the Mortons' two girls experienced almost every type of educational setting: public school, homeschool, and private school. She says as adults they turned out to be articulate, able to form great arguments, and enjoy discussing a variety of topics.

Sometimes people want to know what she and her husband did to make their children so articulate — and most don't expect her simple answer, "We took them places and they read a lot. It wasn't like any big program that we did with them."

She says that while they were purposeful as parents their approach wasn't nearly as intense as what she witnessed when her daughter was enrolled in an international school with a high number of Asian students. "They started students in the boarding school at second grade so that they'd be guaranteed a spot in high school in this particular school that they wanted to be at." Pam says, "I know back in the 1800s that was very common, but now to put a seven-year-old in a year-round boarding school — it's just crazy. I couldn't believe it."

But that's a reality in a world where parents want assurance that they can do something now to make sure their kids will be counted among the best and brightest in the future. "The parents ask, 'With the classes that they're in (second, third, or fourth grade), will they be ready for Harvard?'" Pam says, "Literally, they ask about Harvard. And a couple of the other prestigious schools."

Unfortunately, Pam says it seems like some of the forces she's trying to fight in Egypt and Northern Africa are gaining a foothold back home. A 30-year veteran teacher from Michigan recently joined Educan. "She said it's very much the same thing that she had experienced [in the United States]." Pam says, "It was getting more and more pressure to perform, perform, perform for the test whereas learning was less emphasized. And we know for sure in our part of the world, Egypt, Sudan, Tanzania, it's the same thing. It's pressure."

Pam Morton is the author of One Plane Ticket from Normal: Your Humorous and Hope-Filled Guide to Life in the Middle East.

Chapter Review

Academic competition is driving massive amounts of spending globally. However, in many cases the results don't justify the amount of investment students, parents and governments are making. Meanwhile, test prep replaces opportunities kids should have to explore their world.

PART 2

IGNITE A PASSION FOR LIFE: 7 STEPS TO INSPIRE YOUR CHILD

PRESCRIBING CREATIVITY

"We have to recognize that human flourishing is not a mechanical process. It's an organic process. And you cannot predict the outcome of human development. All you can do is, like a farmer, create the conditions under which they will begin to flourish.

Ken Robinson, Bring on the learning revolution! Ted Talk

"When I grow up I'm going to open a restaurant and I'm going to call it Leafy's." My daughter announced a couple of months before her sixth birthday, "Because some grownups actually *like* to eat salad. But we won't make the kids eat salad." She glanced at her brother's fast-food meal across the table, "We'll give them burgers with only ketchup and pickles."

She went on to detail extensive plans for her future fast food empire including hiring "team captains" to make sure the workers know what they should all be doing. ("That way I can go start more restaurants.") She also planned to give the team captains "bags of extra money to give out to the workers when they do an extra good job." She added that, "The team captains should give out the bags of money instead of me so the workers will really like them…"

I have *literally* heard about the development of Leafy's for *hours*. I have been known to interrupt this vital planning with things like eating, brushing teeth and going to bed. But it remains a fascinating discovery process to find out who my child is — and what she is capable of without placing a painfully heavy burden of academic expectation on a small child's shoulders. (We have no qualms about other types of expectations. Like, "No feet on the table kids." Really, who knew keeping one's feet off the tabletop would be such a weighty responsibility?)

One of the most interesting families I've read about went through this process with their children in the 1970s, before homeschooling was even an accepted educational subculture. David and Micki Colfax built their homestead in Northern California with their four young sons working alongside them and learning through the process. The former professor and teacher provided a book-rich environment, but didn't push their children. They say children, "will learn, will aspire to excellence, if we recognize and respect their different interests and abilities and give them a chance to develop them."[30] Their oldest son learned to read when he was 9 years old — and later graduated from Harvard Medical School. In fact, their three oldest children all graduated from Harvard with honors.

In their book, *Homeschooling for Excellence*, they also recognized the role family legacy played in their children's experience:

"Our program reflected in what one homeschooler called its 'practical bookishness,' our academic and ranch experiences, and well served our boys when it came time to apply to colleges. Had we been homeschoolers who had been, say, boat builders, musicians, or artists, it would have been different in at least some respects — and almost certainly less

conventionally college-preparatory. Perhaps Grant would have by now become a master boat builder, Drew a sophomore at Julliard, and Reed a sculptor."

This approach to education, sometimes called "unschooling", couldn't be more different than the common approach to cram for China's Gaokao exam. And, yet, in a world where all kids are pushed to compete on an international stage, more unconventional methods become increasingly attractive.

It's telling that the all-time most popular TED Talk — 47,094,734 views as of this writing — is entitled "Do schools kill creativity?" In his brilliant presentation, Sir Ken Robinson observes that, "The whole system of public education around the world is a protracted process of university entrance. And the consequence is that many highly talented, brilliant, creative people think they're not because the thing they were good at in school wasn't valued or actually stigmatized."[31]

The effects of such stigmatization seemed apparent when I accepted volunteer opportunities to work with children. In their childish ignorance, 3 year olds were, for the most part, confident and creative storytellers, painters, organizers, and little executives. In contrast, kindergarteners were much easier to manage, but there was something off. I later realized that, as a group, the kindergarteners just didn't seem as smart as their younger counterparts. Perhaps this totally unscientific observation was merely a fluke? Quite possibly. But perhaps there's more to the story. Perhaps what we should fear most is the heavy load of expectations we place on what at child can and can't do at any particular age.

My grandfather once told my mother, "We thought you were so smart before you went to school." What if she really was and only struggled for 12 years due to poor timing? Due to getting the rare lousy teacher for the first six grades? Due to arriving just in time for the great "sight reading" and "new math" experiment? What if thinking Dr. Seuss books were silly caused her to be written off as "too difficult to teach." (I know from a lifetime of learning under her guidance that she has a brilliant mind.)

One thing is certain, concerns that persuaded David and Micki Colfax to keep their kids home in the '70s, and convinced my mother to join a fledgling homeschool movement in the '80s remain just as valid today.

In this section, I'll take you inside the world I grew up in as I was educated at home from Kindergarten through the 12th grade. Homeschooling is an educational movement that's grown from about 10,000 students in the 1970s to an estimated two million students in the United States today — and it's gaining traction in countries all over the world.[32]

Like any human endeavor, it has had its struggles, challenges, and flawed players. But for the most part this educational experiment has been a stunning success — surprising even many of its most passionate pioneers. In the following pages we'll meet some parents and students who not only have fascinating stories to tell, but also have some solid advice for those of us preparing our children to face a challenging world.

AN EDUCATION IN LIFE

In their book *Hard Times in Paradise* David and Micki Colfax tell the incredible story of how standing up for what they believed in got David blacklisted as a professor prompting them to leave behind the world of academia in order to protect their young sons. Incredibly, choosing to live off the land in remote Northern California turned out to be the best possible education. Years later, three of their four sons would graduate from Harvard. But perhaps their greatest legacy is expressed through the stories in their book — both heartbreaking and hilarious — showing how every member of the family pulled together in their struggle for survival.[33]

PROFILE
Bradley Fish: Done with College and Debt-Free

In an age when many young adults struggle to afford college, complete their degrees, and find a job afterward, Bradley Fish has it all. He managed to graduate at age 18 and pay his parents for his $13,000 education the following year.

His ability to blaze through an online college program and complete a couple of internships in the time most teens complete high school surprised even his parents.

His dad, Paul, says, "I wouldn't say that if you had asked us five years ago 'What are we going to do for our kids' college education?' we could have mapped out what has happened."

They started out by having Bradley take a College Level Examination Program (CLEP) test to prove that he was getting a solid high school education at home.

Paul says it was a, "Way for us to have a little piece of paper to wave at somebody if they said 'Did your son really get an A in biology?' And I can go back and I can say 'Well, he passed the college level placement exam for biology.' At that point, everybody is going to say, 'Well, ok. I guess he learned it.'"

But after their son passed that first exam Paul says he and his wife, Tori, started to consider new possibilities, "If he can do it with this, what else can he do it with?"

Paul says "it" turned out to be about, "Half of your college education without much trouble."

The result was a fast-tracked college education that Paul says, "Speeds things up in a hurry and does so in a way that is keeping with the spirit of the education while it may not do it exactly the way everybody else does."

Bradley, who is the oldest of 10 children, seems to be paving the way for his younger siblings. Tori says, "Our 4-year-old right now likes to play that she's doing college. It just becomes part of the culture of our family that, you know, 'Sure, you can do this.'" However, Tori is quick to point out that, "They're all very different and we want to be sensitive to what each of them is called to do and what their strengths and weaknesses are."

In fact, two of Bradley's younger sisters have completed online degrees by the ages of 20 and 21, but through different colleges than their older brother chose. Rather than creating a formula for their children to follow, the family is identifying tools that will give each child some great options for his or her future. They say that flexibility is a key benefit homeschooling offers, "You're just on a conveyor belt going through (in public school). We don't want to do that with our kids. We want to be much more personalized."

Part of Bradley's, and his sisters', success might just be their parents' willingness to look at the world a little differently. Paul and Tori are both college graduates, but Paul says they keep the importance of academic accomplishments in perspective, "We both came to the conclusion that while you certainly probably have more knowledge than the average person in the field that you studied in college it would probably be a stretch to say it was really worth all the time and money that you put into it to learn that stuff versus what you actually use in your life."

As a result, they look for practical ways to make sure their kids learn as much as possible regardless of educational norms. Paul says, "If you just think about it, rather than go through the cookie-cutter approach that everybody else does, when you look at, let's just say, high school chemistry — it's not that much different than college general chemistry so why not do them both?" Instead he says, "Just teach your children some college level chemistry by that age. As long as you have taught them how to teach themselves that's not a big chore."

It's a strategy Bradley's parents will likely implement many times. But both say over the years they've realized that getting ahead academically isn't even what matters most. In fact, even academic success is a result of working to share their values with their children.

"When you look at the top benefits of homeschooling," Paul says, "I think, ironically, it has very little to do with schooling. I think the top benefits of homeschooling have to do with your ability to teach your children how to live as a Christian in this world. It may have very little to do with academics."

Tori agrees that sharing their faith and a life together has become something she treasures, "My adult children are some of my closest friends now and I look forward to that with the ones who are still young."

And while homeschooling may seem like a foreign concept to many modern families, Tori credits it with bringing her family together, "To me, one of the very top benefits about homeschooling is just all about relationships and I don't think that the level of closeness that I have with my children would be possible if they were away from me for eight hours every day."

It's hard for parents to guess what the future will hold, but Tori says they have a simple plan, "To keep doing what we feel is most important for our children." She says others can also do that by, "Every day deciding to take care of your children in the sense of 'What do they really need?' 'What does their soul need to be trained that day?'"

Bradley Fish is an instructor for ronpaulcurriculum.com, an online homeschool education program.

FREE CLASSES FROM THE WORLD'S BEST COLLEGES

Students who want to explore college course offerings can now take free online courses from some of the most prestigious colleges and universities in the world including MIT, Harvard, Berkeley, Princeton, Oxford, and numerous other institutions all over the world.

The website, edX.org, was founded by Harvard and MIT in 2012 and now has 90 partners. Through a partnership with Arizona State University, edX students also have an option to take part in the online "Global Freshman Academy" where they can earn university credits at a fraction of the normal cost — and only pay after they know they have passed the course to reduce the financial risk. (There is a $49 registration fee for the "verified track" so students are eligible for credit after the course is finished.)

The program is open to anyone and doesn't require an application or transcript.[34]

CHAPTER REVIEW

Pushing kids too hard and holding them back can have the same devastating result: they may simply lose the desire to learn. In order to raise creative children with a hunger to learn we need to get more creative in how we approach education.

STEP 1: PROTECT THEIR TIME

"All of humanity's problems stem from man's inability to sit quietly in a room alone."

Blaise Pascal, Pensees

In her excellent book, *Organized Simplicity*, Tsh Oxenreider asks a question that haunts me as a parent, "I wonder what our children's memories will be when they reflect on their upbringing — an innocent time full of play and exploration, or the booster seat on the way to ballet practice?"[35]

This isn't to say that there's anything wrong with a dance class, but rather that parents need to rethink following the crowd in a culture that leaves children with only about eight hours of free time each week — including weekends.

Even more importantly can we ever expect our children to develop an appetite for learning if we never allow them the opportunity to get hungry? To ever desire wisdom if we're constantly filling every available moment with a sugary sweet educational dessert, but never creating opportunities for them to make space for the main course?

As much as they need a healthy balanced diet, kids also need time to think and process the complexities of this world we live in. They need some silence for the same reasons silence is expected in libraries, classrooms, and offices. But we must fight for that as a noisy world invades every aspect of our lives.

Protecting their time is the single most important thing we can do to nourish our children's minds and souls. As we provide opportunities for time with minimal external structure, we allow them to develop essential internal structure.

In fact, German psychologists have found, "a significant positive correlation between ample time for free play during childhood and adult social success." The researchers also noticed that, "Free time as kids was also linked with high self-esteem and the flexibility to adjust one's goals."[36]

Looking back Bradley Fish appreciates the way his parents dialed back their busy lifestyle to create more margin in their routine:

> "When I was young all of us were in soccer teams and that sort of thing growing up and then it got to a point where if you weren't careful we were busy every night of the week and not just for one kid, but maybe multiple kids had things going on each night of the week and when mom and dad decided to pull out of that it didn't create frustration on our part. We enjoyed all those different things, but it was much more important to us, and even more enjoyable, to have a little bit of free time to ourselves or time to spend with our family."

Bradley adds that a more relaxed schedule actually, "Turned out to be good and beneficial to us rather than, even as kids, trying to chase that rat race."

Kathy Hirsh-Pasek, Ph.D., co-author of "Einstein Never Used Flashcards" writes that kids, "need time to recharge their batteries and process what they've learned. Free time allows them to explore, to be scientists, discoverers, creators, and innovators. They do that when they build pillow forts in the family room, sail away in a laundry basket to a foreign land, or find the remarkable in the mundane."[37]

Taking a similar approach to that of the Fish family, Pastor Dave Gross says providing plenty of free time was a key component in how he and his wife, Kay, home educated their three children. They made daily time together a priority by reading a Bible story, discussing what they read, and having the kids finish their core-subject school work by noon each day. They wanted their kids to, "Be creative, to be thinking, to be coming up with their own things to do and games to play."

That meant they never played on sports teams or took dance classes. After a few years, music lessons were dropped when it became apparent music wasn't a passion of theirs. A homeschool group meeting a couple of hours each week and a weekly "Little Rangers" program at church provided time to socialize with other kids.

At home, Dave says they had all the tools necessary for endless hours of adventurous play as they grew, "I had all kinds of things like knives and hatchets and go karts and motorbikes, bicycles, and you name it when it came to play... When it came time to teach our kids how to drive a car we didn't need to teach them because they'd driven around on three acres of land on a go kart so long that it was all natural to them."

Dave says that approach provided plenty of time to, "Let them be kids and play and enjoy life." And he says those opportunities prepared them well for the rest of their lives.

When we hear stories like this it sounds so simple, yet passing on organized play dates, turning down chances to participate in sports, and skipping opportunities to take extracurricular classes are probably some of the most difficult decisions for modern parents to make. The problem is that we find it difficult to say "no" to good things in order to make space for the best things. Yet choosing to say "yes" to every great opportunity that comes along is, in essence, saying "no" to you and your child's best possible life. Author Sally Clarkson put it this way: "Although our culture seems to worship being busy, constant activity will slowly undermine our perspective on life and kill our souls."

I have found that a busy life is not only soul-killing, but that quiet hours are life-giving — fueling a child's passion for life and forming a mind that's constantly absorbing truth about the world.

Sarah Mackenzie is another homeschooling author and blogger I love to follow. In her book, *Teaching from Rest*, she tells about learning the Latin meaning of the word *rigor*, "which means 'numbness, stiffness, hardness, firmness, roughness, rudeness.' 'Rigor mortis' literally means 'the stiffness of death.'"[38] That's probably not exactly what parents have in mind when it comes to giving their children a rigorous education!

Instead Mackenzie's mentors encouraged her to cultivate diligence in her children:

> *"'Diligence' comes from the Latin diligere which means to 'single out, value highly, esteem, prize, love; aspire to, take delight in, appreciate.' What we are really aiming for in giving our children a rigorous education is not just doing hard things, but cultivating a habit of focused attention. The word "student" comes from the Latin stadium, meaning "zeal, affection, eagerness.' A diligent student, then, takes delight eagerly and with great zeal, in what he loves."*

Developing the "focused attention" diligence requires is essential if we hope to raise kids who are not only smart, but also are prepared to use their knowledge to "do the right thing" in every situation. And that takes time.

ONE ON ONE TIME

Parenting expert Amy McCready says "Mind, Body and Soul Time" is critical to provide the emotional connection kids crave. She says it's also the, "most effective means of reducing negative attention-seeking behaviors."[39] So how does it work? McCready encourages parents to set aside two 10-minute chunks of time each day to be fully available to each child in the family. You can learn more in her temptingly titled book, *If I Have to Tell You One More TIME... The Revolutionary Program That Gets Your Kids to Listen Without Nagging, Reminding, or Yelling.*

A FASHION EMPIRE BUILT ON BOREDOM

Sometimes even boredom can be an asset — just ask Bethany Mota. She's built a media and fashion empire that's caught the attention of the business world. Sarah Lybrand told her story for Yahoo Finance in 2014:

> *"Now with her own clothing line at retailer Aeropostale, Bethany's rising stardom goes far beyond her 'MACBARBIE07' — a YouTube channel that's generating an estimated $40,000 per month and has garnered over 300 million views since she launched it. She is an inspiration to pre-teens everywhere who've ever struggled with boredom, shyness and bullying."[40]*

Lynbrand reported that Bethany was homeschooled until junior high when she entered public school, but pulled out of the school system after experiencing cyber-bullying. "Bored, lonely and looking for an outlet, she redirected her energy into an unexpected hobby: creating YouTube videos for girls just like her that offered make-up tips and fashion advice, among other things."

According to Lyndbrand's story about five years after her YouTube debut, Bethany had, "more than 5.5 million channel subscribers and 2.4 million fans on Instagram. That's more than Vogue, Elle, Marie Claire, Glamour and Cosmopolitan combined."

PROFILE
Erica Foster: Teaching Through Tough Times

When, as a pastor's wife, Erica Foster started homeschooling her third grade son she never could have imagined that she would ultimately end up teaching — and raising — five children alone.

As a single mom, Erica relies on her faith, but at times it can be difficult to cope with her situation in Christian social circles, "Sometimes it's just in my head maybe but I do feel a lot of judgmental viewpoints from people especially from very conservative families where they're very strict on things — and they're against divorce no matter what. It doesn't matter what the situation is it."

Yet she says becoming an outcast in social circles where her family used to be fully accepted has also been a great learning experience, "It's just kind of caused us to grow in our relationship with Christ and knowing who we are and we didn't choose the path that we're on and we just have to keep going."

Erica says the decision to keep teaching her kids as a single mom is something she's questioned nearly every year, "Then I say, 'No. God showed me that if I put my children first, training and discipling them he will always provide for me.' And it's true that every time that I... decide to go do it on my own strength it fails but when I just trust God and training them and discipling the best way that I can He does. He continues to provide and there's harmony in our family and peace — and I can enjoy my children as a single mom."

Over the years, more than the family dynamic has changed. Erica knew she wanted to homeschool even as she sent her oldest son to kindergarten, first, and second grade.

She says, "I was married at the time when I started. My husband wasn't really for it at first but he started seeing great results with other children and he knew my heart." After their son experienced a year learning very little under a particularly harsh teacher, her husband came to her saying he thought it was time they started homeschooling.

Their first month was a strict classroom setting with their third grade son and his kindergarten-aged little sister, "My former husband wanted to have them wear uniforms. They had to be in their seats at 8 o'clock with their uniforms on, their hair combed — and that lasted about one month."

With two younger children in the house, Erica says maintaining a "real school" setting soon became too much, "And that's when I started to really start researching. It is important for them to have those habits of waking up and doing their chores and getting dressed but to have that pressure of being in their seats at 8 o'clock with their uniforms on was quite overwhelming."

Ultimately, she says she discovered that, "They learned better when it was more relaxed and they were learning through teachable moments and we still had a set curriculum but most of their learning was when they were more relaxed."

At the same time, she started researching education methods going back to the 1800s and says what she discovered was, "Unbelievable. Greek, Latin, they had memorized hundreds of poems and scriptures — and their education was just amazing."

She remembers reading an old eighth grade test and struggling to imagine an eighth grader being able to pass it now. "It made me just realize they use Scripture all the time," She says, "And the Scripture's alive. It's living. It's getting that in their heart."

That realization made her think more deeply about her real goals for her children's education, "Our goal as parents is to raise godly children." She says, "Not just smart children but full of God's character."

As a result, over the rocky years that followed, the family spent lots of time learning through reading, including reading out loud, and memorizing.

Once she found herself raising her kids as a single home-schooling mom, Erica joined a local Classical Conversations teaching co-op. She says she did it because, as a single parent, she liked having the accountability of having her kids participate in a structured program. She was also able to be a tutor for the program and make money while her kids attended for free.

She's says it also provided an opportunity for her kids to experience a competitive setting — and for her to help them process how to deal with it. When there was a focus on which student would be the best at Memory Master she told them, "You know if you want to go for that I want to challenge you to do that, but I don't want you to lose sleep over it."

One of the biggest concerns many people have with homeschooling is whether kids will get enough experience socializing with others their own age. While some of Erica's kids have had spent some time going to schools, for the most part they've been homeschooled. And she says even without going to school daily they experience plenty of positive and negative social interactions.

With a house full of teens and preteens, she says it's important to talk about and through any situations they find difficult. "It is good to have negative [experiences] at times because you don't want to shield your kids." She says, "You want them to ask questions and learn." She adds that it's also important to make sure they don't become overwhelmed with difficult social situations. "There is a time when there can be so much of the negative it starts pulling them down." Erica says, "And that's where as a parent you need to be looking out for that... and helping to guard their hearts. A lot of times they don't even see it they're in it so much."

Weathering life's storms is something Erica has plenty of experience going through with her children. The heartbreak of divorce and having their father completely out of their lives for several years and mourning the death of Erica's father made it hard to focus on academics. Erica says that at times she worries whether in the future they will look back and say, "Mom, you never taught me this. It's all your fault!"

But she's also noticed that learning at home is extremely efficient, "You learn so much faster in your own home within 2 hours than you can with 25 to 30 students in a whole month." So in the end she's just working to make the right decisions for her children one year at a time and, most importantly, "Just building a relationship with them and just enjoying them."

Erica Foster shares more of her story in "You Taught My Feet to Dance" telling her readers, "what happens when God's relentless love collides with your deepest human desperation."

REVIEW
Steps to Inspire Your Children

1. Protect their time: Children need time to explore their world and learn to become quietly comfortable with themselves.

STEP 2: SET EXPECTATIONS

*"My contention is that all kids have tremendous talents
and we squander them pretty ruthlessly."*

Ken Robinson, Do Schools Kill Creativity? Ted Talk

"YOU'RE NOT MY TEACHER!" To say that my three-year-old son was uncooperative that morning would be an understatement.

"Yes, I am. I am your mother and Daddy and I can pick your teachers or teach you ourselves."

"Well, teachers don't make people really do things anyway." He pouted.

"Yes, they do. Now sit down and enjoy this."

Eight hours after our 15-minute preschool session my little guy interrupted supper preparations with a hug, "You're a good teacher Mama."

The above exchange represents the number one reason I hear for why many parents won't even consider homeschooling. And I get it. Working with your child one-on-one may seem to make no sense when the same child would likely comply in a classroom setting. Yet, whether you teach your child at home or follow a traditional school route, cultivating a sense of parental authority equips you to become his or her best guidance counselor through the first 18 years of life — and hopefully a best friend thereafter.

Of course, most conversations with my children aren't as blunt as the one above. Spending plenty of time with them naturally deepens our relationship. This means I not only have positional authority derived from my "Mom" title, but I also *am* an authority on my child. I often think of this Proverb when dealing with the complicated little people in my life:

"A plan in the heart of a man is like deep water,
But a man of understanding draws it out."[41]

Things are already starting to get deep when we have to determine whether a young child needs to be prodded along firmly, take a breath of fresh air, or have a nap. That only intensifies as our children grow older. Exerting parental authority is also naturally more confrontational than allowing our children to learn through peer pressure in a group setting. Yet it may also be the reason for solid social skills and self-confidence that represent the best of homeschooling.

As a child, I experienced the group pressure that convinces kids to conform, behave, and avoid any unacceptable behavior that caused me to "stick out" in a social setting. But even more importantly, I was blessed with a wise mother who was genuinely interested in my social life and helped me process any conflicts or uncomfortable situations. That meant I got a jumpstart on learning to intentionally do the right thing for the right reasons — whether or not it was popular in a particular group setting. I am especially impressed when I see my younger sister use this type of judgement as she navigates the business world.

This is the type of relationship we need to cultivate with our children — walking alongside them as they grow — in order equip them to become leaders in the future. But that is also hard work. In fact, Paul Fish says that teaching academic subjects may just be the easiest part of raising children, "Homeschooling is a breeze as compared to the behavior training of your children and disciplining them."

With kids ranging in age from 4 years old to 22 years old, his wife, Tori, says it's work that should start as soon as possible:

"If you don't establish a strong level of discipline in your home from really day one with your children then when it comes time to say, 'Ok, now we're going to sit down and have a math lesson,' your children are not going to be prepared to handle that or respect you. Or get done what needs to be done. So it certainly — even when you're technically not homeschooling those early years — you've got be laying the foundation of 'When Mommy says to do something it's your job to do it and to do it with a happy attitude.'"

And what about kids who have already reached their teen years? Paul says he's observed that parents can still have a positive impact on their kids — it's just even more work, "It's not to say that it's hopeless at that point, but I will say at that point you've got a long hard uphill battle to try and establish what you should have established 10 or 13 years previous."

That work training the heart of our children isn't always going to be appreciated, but Tori says that when kids lash out and push their parents away is when it's most important to dig in and persevere, "Hold on tight to them and keep pushing them and encouraging them in the way that you want them to go. I mean that's our job." Indeed, love is the best hard work we will ever engage in.

Our kids also need to know that we expect them to do well and they need obvious opportunities to fulfill those expectations. Author Pat Broomfield Bradley started teaching her twin daughter and son in the seventh grade. She says they had to learn, "Mom would grade papers and give it back to them and they had to do it over." She says that was a big change from school where you, "just get a grade and it's over with and you go onto the next thing." In fact, one of the strengths of homeschooling is that having the same instructor over several years means students are often called on to not only fully complete their work each year, but also eventually master areas where they tend to struggle.

One of the world's most successful school systems also keeps the same students and teachers working together for many years. Compared to their counterparts in Asia students in Finland spend relatively few hours studying, yet they tend to score well on international standardized tests. One feature of the country's distinctive education system is that students are often kept with the same teacher for up to six years in elementary school — a system that must allow the teachers to continue to build up their student's strengths and work on their weaknesses.[42]

It all sounds so idyllic, especially if you're reading this after the kids are in bed, but what about when the 5-year-old is standing on her head instead of doing her math worksheet, the baby wakes up in the middle of his nap, and the 3-year-old is questioning your ability to handle the entire situation? Well, that's when the real learning happens — and when you'll discover the importance of setting your and your children's expectations for how life and learning work.

Whether you send your kids to school or keep them at home, parenting will be a stressful experience at times. But once you've established a sense of parental authority in your home, you have an environment conducive to reaching your parenting goals. And it's important to have goals set for those days when life with kids threatens to take your focus off what really matters.

I want my children to:

1. *Learn to function under authority and gain skills to appropriately work within authority structures.* This is because I want to raise strong, independent thinkers who will

be taken seriously when they stand up for something they believe in. When they develop tact and communication skills they will be able to share ideas, express their personalities, and maintain their integrity. They will also be equipped to become leaders themselves.

2. *Learn to work for incentive and virtue.* It's often said that kids need to learn "the value of a dollar." My first job — in taxidermy — as a teen probably resonated with that sentiment. I only made a few dollars an hour and spent plenty of time working with half-rotten rabbit hides. That job certainly helped me appreciate every other job thereafter, but I learned the most about money through an office job many years later. As the Donor Relations Officer for a political education and lobbying organization, I spent a lot of time talking to our highest contributing donors. Making phone calls to set up meetings requesting money might not sound like much fun, but I saw it as a chance to spend most of my days talking to amazing people. Many of the wealthiest people seem to understand their own value, create value for their customers, and create value as they give generously. That life-giving attitude toward work is something I'd love to foster in my children's minds and hearts.

3. *Learn fundamental academic skills regardless of interest level — and train themselves to find the interesting in the mundane.* I don't believe education should be overly burdensome, yet there is still great value in preparing our children to accept that every moment of their day won't be super exciting. In a media-rich world that's constantly pushing the envelope to dish up new thrills, it's especially challenging and important to help our kids experience the satisfaction of accomplishing the many mundane tasks essential to almost any significant achievement.

4. *Learn about our culture and other cultures at a deep level through language, literature, food, and experiences.* Just as kids benefit from exposure to a diverse set of classmates and teachers in a traditional school setting, homeschool students also benefit from the relationships they develop at home and in their communities. Reading aloud, shopping and cooking together, and community volunteer projects all offer opportunities to experience the richness, color, and depth of our world.

5. *Learn the true meaning and practice of love.* This is the most important item on this list. We hear a lot about the importance of "socialization" from the time children are old enough to be sent to daycare. Yet with nearly a half of all marriages ending in divorce it seems that we as a nation (indeed, based on the news, the entire world) could stand a bit of work on our interpersonal relationships.

6. *Grow physically, mentally, and emotionally resilient.* It's not enough to try to create a "safe world" for our kids, they also need to spend their time growing strong and healthy in every way so that when they're forced to face the "real world" they are truly prepared.

If these expectations seem vague it's because they were intentionally designed to be so. I agree with home educating dad Dave Gross, profiled later in this book, who says parents' expectations are "one of the most dangerous things for raising good kids." There's no greater burden for children than the pressure to compensate for their parents' own regrets, disappointments, and failures. Yet having no expectations at all for our children is like setting them afloat in rough seas with no navigation skills. Successful homeschool parents are adept at helping their children reach their true potential without giving into the temptation to force their own dreams onto their children.

INTENTIONAL PARENTING

In his excellent book *Intentional Living* John Maxwell says:

> *"As parents Margaret and I realized when our children were young that we couldn't teach them everything so we came up with five essential principles we wanted to pass along and help them be successful and feel about who they are. We wanted to ground them in faith, responsibility, unconditional love, gratitude, and self-worth. We included self-worth because we understood that it is impossible to consistently behave in a way that is inconsistent with how we feel about ourselves on the inside. Self-image dictates daily behavior. How we see ourselves regulates what we consistently do, and our regular behavior is what defines us, not what we might do on a rare occasion."* [43]

PROFILE
Pat Broomfield Bradley: Faith Academy

Pat Broomfield Bradley's son was tested and labeled as a gifted learner — one who was flunking sixth grade. Realizing that he needed more of a challenge, Pat and her husband pulled him and his twin sister out of public school and put them in a Christian private school with an accelerated learning program.

That meant the family was now forking over money for five tuitions as Pat had just returned to school to finish her degree, her husband was in graduate school, and her oldest daughter had already started college. No surprise Pat was also working two jobs to keep everything afloat.

But after graduating from Texas Woman's University, she soon found herself out of school and without a job, "I said, 'Well Lord, this is something I know you wanted.'" She says, "The Lord had told me in the first place, in my spirit, that 'I want you to write advertising for me I want you to be *my* PR.'"

Realizing she couldn't afford to keep her twins in private school any longer she decided she could — and would — homeschool. Even when Liberty Christian School offered to provide scholarships, she decided to bring her twins home and so began, "Five years of adventure for us."

In Texas, it was easy to find a huge homeschooling book fair where she was able to browse curriculum and order what she thought looked best, "I just went into full preparation mode. I got the books and in time I went through them myself preparing lesson plans and preparing syllabi so that you know we could stay on track and that's how I got started." Her husband was skeptical and neighbors told her she was crazy, "They thought I was off my loony bin and I had relatives telling me, 'You must be out of your mind.'"

But before long, her husband threw his support behind the effort, "I'd say about a month into homeschooling he had to go to Arizona to complete one of his projects and he called me one night while he was out in Arizona, I think it was Phoenix, and he was so excited." A local news station had featured a story about a mother who had home schooled her children through high school. Then she and her two children entered the University of Arizona. At graduation, the mother and her two children claimed the top three spots in their class. Pat says her husband suddenly saw the potential in their new family venture.

After that, her husband was enthusiastically telling everyone about their approach, "He was just so supportive and he was just the proud homeschooling papa you know telling everybody we're home schooling like it was his idea, well, the Lord got him on board!"

Pat says that from that time forward homeschooling was a good experience for her family. However, she says it's an undertaking nobody should approach lightly, "This is a full time job and it is a commitment and you have to look at it in a structured fashion."

She recommends structuring the school with a legal name. Her family's was called Faith Academy. She also organized the kids' classes using a similar structure to college classes with classes offered on Mondays, Wednesdays, and Fridays or on Tuesdays and Thursdays. That made it easier for the kids to have dedicated blocks of time to focus on each subject rather than trying to fit five or six subjects into their schedule on a daily basis. She says that schedule, "Enabled them to concentrate and to really absorb the information better." She also created a syllabus with content and expectations for each subject.

Even though they built a lot of structure into their school program, the family also took advantage of the flexibility to travel during the school year. Since her husband traveled a lot for work they would often, "Just pack up the books and get in the van and go with him."

Pat says she also spent plenty of time during those critical teen years sharing her values with the twins, "We are a Christian family and one of the things that the twins and I would do is have Bible study before we began our school work each morning. We taught them that they should always consult the Lord about what they were to do and His will and calling for them in life."

After graduating from high school at home, Pat's son went to the University of Missouri on a full scholarship where he majored in computer science. He's now an IT instructor for the US Coast Guard in California and his twin sister is a digital librarian and program planner in Colorado. She has her master's degree from Rutgers University in library information and science.

Pat says, "A lot of people will tell you, or try to make you fear, that your child's chances of going to college after being homeschooled are very slim and that is so far from the truth." She adds, "Because your child is homeschooled the colleges will be more interested in them simply because they have, out of their experience of admitting and dealing with other homeschool students, found them to be better prepared, more committed, and just better students. I've had them tell me this."

Perhaps equally important as academic skills, are the practical daily life skills Pat insisted that her children learn, "During the time that they were growing up I required that they also learned the living skills such as household chores: how to clean the house, how to do laundry, how to cook meals, and all this kind of stuff." She laughs now when she recalls those days, "During that time, that learning process, my children were actually telling people I had re-institutionalized slavery." However she says all that hard work was eventually appreciated, "Every last one of them, all three of them have called me at different times and thanked me for teaching them how to take care of themselves."

Pat Broomfield Bradley is the author of the Under His Shadow series. Her most recent volume, "The Light Bearers: Witnesses of the Redeeming Love and Amazing Grace that's Available for you" is available wherever books are sold.

REVIEW
Steps to Inspire Your Children

1. Protect their time: Children need time to explore their world and learn to become quietly comfortable with themselves.

2. Set Expectations: Children need to know that their parents expect them to do well and they need opportunities to prove it.

Step 3: Let Them Dream

"The important thing is not so much that every child should be taught, as that every child should be given the wish to learn."

John Lubbock

It was a gorgeous June morning with sunshine and patches of green on rolling hills. A beautiful time of year in our high desert landscape. Birds darted around, dipping low near the water in an irrigation canal that creates a sort of summer fowl sanctuary behind our home. My 20-month-old little boy pressed his sweet babyish face against a window pane. *"I wish I could fly."* His wish was expressed in a clear, wistful tone.

Apparently, dreams are not only the stuff of youth and childhood, but even toddlerhood. And they are so important. Dreams are the seeds of creativity, innovation, and noble aspirations. But what happens when the demands of life crowd in? Marking items off developmental checklists can nearly become an obsession with my generation of parents. Will our children be the first generation too busy becoming "well-rounded" to press their noses against glass letting their minds, and imaginations, wander and wonder what is in that big world outside? What happens when that becomes the case?

I think we end up with parents breathlessly carting their children to overpriced classes designed to help children express their creativity — by making some art project or participating in some activity in conformity with a room full of their peers. We end up with a society that worships the *idea* of unique individuality without even being able to comprehend the sacred value of each and every human soul.

But is there really time to allow our children to be lost in dreamland while their peers begin intense academic training as preschoolers? Yes. I firmly believe we can nurture our children's minds and prepare them for life, but also leave space for them to explore — and even help fuel their imaginations.

Writing for psychologytoday.com, Timothy A. Pychyl, Ph.D. argues that inspiration is even an essential component in the learning process. As an educator, Pychyl adheres to the concept that "Education is not the filling of a pail, but the lighting of a fire."[44] In fact, as someone who studies procrastination scientifically, he compares the three elements needed to start a fire (fuel, heat, and air) with the three fundamental human needs identified by researchers who developed something called "Self-Determination Theory." That theory, developed by Richard Ryan and Edward Deci, holds that there are three fundamental human needs for motivation: competence, autonomy, and relatedness. Pychyl states the case even more concisely saying that you need both "will and skill" in order to "light a fire for learning."

And, as every parent or educator knows, the fire for learning can be incredibly different from one child to another. As Pychyl writes, there's a huge difference between trying to manage an explosive wildfire and dealing with what seems like a "soggy log." Some fires do have to be "gently nurtured from the remnants of glowing coals or from accessing the inner dry wood in what appears to be a soggy log." But success is still possible.

So, what does any of this have to do with giving our children opportunities to dream? Well, according to researchers, interest is actually an emotion. And, as every parent knows, teaching our children how to manage their emotions is one of our most important tasks. For anyone with a toddler, it's abundantly obvious that we need to help them learn how to manage emotions like anger, excitement, and fear. We also want to teach them to develop a sense of compassion and concern for other people. Likewise, our ability to help our children develop and manage a healthy interest in the world around them is likely to significantly affect them for the rest of their lives.

Keeping her kids interested in the world — and all they can learn from books — is something homeschool mom Mystie Winckler aims to do. In the process, she's noticed that English educator Charlotte Mason was right about how children learn, "The thing Charlotte Mason said that I doubted the most before I had kids was that children want to know kind of innately and they have curiosity — we can mess up their curiosity — but they have it to begin with."

Mystie and her husband are second-generation homeschoolers. Mystie says the opportunity for plenty of free reading time — and the desire to do it — was one of the greatest things they gained as students.

"I think we had just started out and I think we were talking about what we wanted our homeschool to look like," Mystie says when her husband recalled the benefit of books *not* assigned, "He said that of all the things that he read or learned when he was homeschooled what he still remembered is the information from the books that he chose to read himself, not the books that were assigned to him."

As a result, Mystie says they find ways to provide their children with plenty of books and make time available for reading rather than focusing on assigning specific books they think are important. It's all part of an effort to, "Keep that atmosphere of just preferring having lots of books and lots of time for free reading over assigning books that we think are important." Mystie says choosing not to simply work through a list of reading assignments makes it a lot more difficult to measure what her kids are learning, "but it's a beautiful thing."

Teacher and reading coach Michael Myers also agrees that sparking the imagination can be the foundation for a great education, "The way you get kids passionate about learning is that you help them learn about what they're interested in and it's not always about learning about what we have to learn about that day — that's just a killer." Michael says that some of the best teachers in his district know how give the kids space to cultivate their interests, "They do projects where it's not about trying to master this content but it's more about trying to master a way to present the content — how to organize the content. So you have kids giving a 'how to' speech or giving more information about popcorn, about how to fix a radiator or something."

Michael says this interest-based learning can also be used to help motivate students even when they have to master a task they don't find interesting, "You can help them apply the skills from their interest learning to what they have to learn about. And then celebrate their victories and praise them for it and let them know what they're doing well specifically." Michael says, adding that you should also, "Let them know how they can improve specifically."

Most importantly, Myers says the "easiest things to leave out in learning" are emotions and considering how a child is feeling — and yet there's a lot of power in harnessing that aspect of learning.

"When we say 'passion' we mean energy that motivates us — that pushes us to do something, right?" Myers says, then he concludes that it's, "Love that pushes us to do something."

PLAYING ON PURPOSE

Two moms have taken preschool play to a whole new level forming a company called "The Home Grown Preschooler."

Their flagship product is a beautiful book called "A Year of Playing Skillfully."[45] With expertise in education and special needs, they make a compelling case for emphasizing play and regular sensory stimulation noting that brain cells that aren't used are eventually shed to make the brain work more efficiently. Find out more at www.tericapshaw.com/dyingtowin.

HOMESCHOOL MVP

Heisman Trophy winner and former professional NFL quarterback Tim Tebow is the youngest of five children who were taught at home from kindergarten through graduating from high school. His parents, "planned each child's schooling around their family values, character training, and the individual's learning style, interests, and goals."[46]

In his area, Tebow could participate in school athletics while doing his academic work at home. He started getting national media attention even as a high school student.

Today, "Tim Tebow" bills, which allow homeschool students to participate in public school extra curricular activities, have been made into law in or are being considered in several states.[47]

PROFILE
Jen Cole: Turning a Ravenous Learner Loose

Jen Cole likes to joke that her son Matthew could, "Take a watch, hit it with a hammer, throw it in the air, and tell you what time it is when he looks up." She says his gift is being a, "Global thinker to such and extreme he takes a whole problem at once and creates a solution."

On the other hand, Jen describes herself as, "Extremely linear and sequential in my thinking. I move my thinking from point A to point B so the mastery approach just feels right to me. You start with one fact and you build on it and build on it and keep moving in one direction.

Jen says she, "knew [Matthew] was different" since he was young. After all, it's not exactly normal for a 4-year-old to routinely solve complicated algebraic story problems while on a drive in the car. That was confirmed when, many years later, a confetti-filled tube arrived at their house with an early enrollment certificate from MIT — one of only 314 the top-ranking university in the world sends out each year. (I know, all you math people got the "pi" tie-in right away while the rest of us were wondering why they didn't pick a nice, round number.) MIT proved to be a good fit with Matthew opting to take the graduate level aerospace exit project rather than following the standard undergraduate path.

After graduation, he found himself going to work for the government and returning to the naval base that his parents took him to as a seven week old baby as they awaited his father's assignment.

His mother says she is not surprised that he got the job he wanted, "He's lucky, but he makes his own luck."

These days, some parents are dreaming of top tier colleges when their little ones are still in diapers, but Jen says Matthew was in ninth grade when she began to believe that he was positioning himself for a top university.

Despite his obviously unusual aptitude for math as a pre-schooler, Matthew led a normal life as a busy little boy. "He was a kid that had energy to burn." Jen remembers, "Man, that kid, he was exhausting from the second he woke up."

Matthew's early education was fairly normal. He attended a small Catholic school from Kindergarten through third grade. He learned to read when he was six and was always leading his class. Then in third grade he took his first standardized tests, "He was always in the 99th percentile in every subject." Jen says, "The 99th percentile just means you took the wrong test — there's nothing higher than that."

After that, a move forced them to look for a new school. Jen says that she and her husband had heard about homeschooling, and one day she had "one of those big moments with the light bulb going off" and realized homeschooling might be a good option.

She says she was a bit reluctant to start, "Homeschool wasn't a 'thing' in the late 90s. Everybody wore a jeans jumper and knee socks. It was really hard for me to agree to do it." But in the end she decided to give this counter-culture approach a shot (while keeping her own fashion sense intact).

She homeschooled Matthew for the fourth, fifth, and sixth grades.

When she started out with him in the fourth grade, she says she handed him an Apologia science middle school textbook. He had a 95% score at the end of the year. For fifth grade she gave him the next book, Physical Science. "And I started to panic part way through that year," she says, worried that "he was going to run out of things to do. So I held him back."

In retrospect, she says she realizes that initially she held him back a lot because she was afraid he would get so far ahead that she wouldn't be able to properly record his work for his transcript. She says those were back in the days when she thought she had to be "perfect in every way", then she and her husband reached a realization that they were holding him back merely for paperwork.

She says his desire to learn was like, "Having 24 broncos attached to the Red Ryder [wagon] — and I just let him go at some point."

She says she came to learn that, "Matthew just doesn't, and didn't, need hours to get a thing learned." Some school years homeschooling he completed as many as 12 subjects in homeschool and he was still done before his brother and sister who are two years and five years younger than him.

Incredibly, she says, "He was never mentally exhausted."

Then he attended the seventh grade at a Department of Defense school in Japan where the family had been relocated for her husband's job. Part of her goal was to start documenting his credits for high school.

However, she hit a road block when it came to enrolling him for classes in the eighth grade. Jen recalls a memorable meeting where, "A school counselor told me that Matthew couldn't be as gifted as I was implying because he wasn't autistic." She says, "It was just beyond one of the dumbest things I've ever heard." At the same meeting, another counselor told her that they couldn't let Matthew take the next class he needed since it was offered at the high school and they wouldn't let him go there to take it. The counselor told her that she should, "Take him to the library more."

She took him home and exclusively homeschooled him for the eighth grade. By the time he was old enough to go to high school for ninth grade he already had 11 high school credits. She says, "And then there was no question he was far and away above his peers."

He made his mark at the Department of Defense high school when he was bored and solved the first derivative before the teacher had given the students the preparatory work for it. The teacher said that was only the second time that had happened in his 30-year teaching career.

"He would read something once and know it and he was usually the teacher's assistant. By the junior year, they had to put him in AP classes, but here at the overseas DoD high schools they didn't have teachers to teach them always so he was distance learning so his junior and senior year he would be in the distance learning lab, otherwise known as the library." She says more than half of his workload involved distance learning.

Despite living in Japan where local students tend to be under intense academic pressure, Jen says Matthew took high school in stride, "He would go to school. He would come home relaxed and happy. The teachers loved him. They would ask him to come down and fix things in the tech lab."

Based on his abilities and natural competitive nature, Jen says Matthew would have likely thrived in any school setting. However this non-traditional route allowed him to complete far more classes than normal — an important factor for applying to MIT — and he managed to do so without the pressure many students face in a typical prep school environment.

"He was always able to work from a position of knowledge and comfort. He didn't have those stresses of, 'You've got to produce. You have to compete. You have to show that you're the top.'" Jen says, "And Matthew didn't have a top edge until he got to MIT."

Jen says she can't really take credit for Mathew's success. While some people tend to assume that a talented student is lazy, Matthew loved to learn. And he soon began to work independently allowing her time to work with her three younger children.

In fact, perhaps her most powerful lesson is that parents need to guard against taking credit for their children's success.

"As a homeschooling mom, I found about my third or fourth year I hit my burn out patch." She says, "You don't even realize that you've gone down the path wearing rose-colored glasses and you believe that you're going to homeschool these little people all the way through and when I had the realization that I had to solve the problem the right way."

The solution ended up being sending one of her kids to a school outside of the home.

She says that was "crushing to my ego" since she was moderating a large, 1,000-member group of Sonlight curriculum users, "It was a big deal to suddenly not be a 100% homeschooler, but, as has happened to me so often in life, as hard as it was for me then, I became the person who could give a pat on the back when another homeschooler realized that they had to put their kids in school for whatever reason."

She says it's important to understand that there are a lot of reasons parents decide to send their kids to school and, "They don't make those decisions lightly. And they cry."

She doesn't want to take any credit from parents who do homeschool all the way — it's just important for parents to realize that they need to make the best decisions for their individual children and families.

She also agrees with some other parents that it's a good idea to sign up homeschooled teens for something like duel enrollment classes, "If you have a student destined for academia you need to let them get out into it." She says, "And you need to let them get some lessons while they're still under your roof."

Since this interview was conducted Jen Cole's family left Japan and now call Virginia home. Jen went back to school to become qualified to teach seventh-12th grade chemistry. She spent a year teaching middle school science. However, she says she believes in homeschooling so much she's currently teaching her youngest son who is in the fifth grade.

REVIEW
Steps to Inspire Your Children

1. Protect their time: Children need time to explore their world and learn to become quietly comfortable with themselves.

2. Set Expectations: Children need to know that their parents expect them to do well and to get opportunities to prove it.

3. Let Them Dream: Inspiration is an essential component in the learning process — so let children explore topics that fascinate them.

STEP 4: TEACH GOAL SETTING

"The view from the finish line changes everything. It begs you to think forward. What will be lost if you don't run the courageous race? Who will be left behind? Who will miss your intended contribution if you don't run for impact?"

Jim Akers, Tape Breakers

One of my favorite oddities, invariably on display at our local fair each summer, are bonsai trees. I've always idly wondered how those adorable perfect specimens are developed as miniature replicas of massive trees. The truth came as a bit of a shock: they are simply normal trees confined to, and meticulously cared for in, tiny pots. This visual provides a sharp reminder of why it matters not only how we care for our children, but also where we plant them. If we want them to grow strong and healthy enough to reach their full potential we must choose fertile ground with space for their roots to spread.

I like to think of dreams as the stuff that helps them reach up — stretching toward the sky — and goal setting as the encouragement to help their roots burrow down deep. A young tree needs plenty of care and water — and yet as it grows it needs some occasional semi-dry spells to encourage its roots to burrow deep into the ground in search of water so that it will be firmly anchored in place when storms sweep over the landscape.

As I write this, my almost 4-year-old son is already engaged in his first bit of difficult, but encouraging hard work straining to meet a serious goal. His sister's own accomplishment at age four looms large in family lore. It helps that we have pictures of her big day.

There was cake, balloons, and a new set of Friends Legos wrapped in craft paper and decorated with metallic stickers. She spent the afternoon running through the apartment performing all kinds of un-princess-like antics in her favorite "princess dress." This party, as she called it, her "100 Party", was all she had dreamed it would be. It also marked the first time she had chosen to do something difficult daily for months in order to reach a specific goal: completing the first 100 lessons in her phonics reading program. That celebration amounted to more than a reward for hard work — it also marked a new level of independence. And a milestone her little brothers are eager to reach as well.

Encouraging goal setting is one of the most powerful tools many homeschool parents deploy — and one any parent can use. The process can take on many different forms. It might be a list with a chart, specific steps, and deadlines. Or it might be tackling a chemistry course essential for a future medical career.

The Fish family takes a casual approach that's proven effective over the years. Mom Tori says, "It's just conversation in our home. It's just kind of — it's deliberate in the sense of I know what I want my kids to know and believe but yet it's just a conversation that occurs throughout the day whether it's talking to them about dreams or goals or how they need to work more diligently on something." She says it's "just something that we live." But it's also a process heavily dependent on time spent developing a close relationship with her children, "I don't think those same things are possible to the same extent if you're not just immersed in life all day together."

Teacher Mike Myers agrees that goal setting and providing encouragement along the way is key. He say each authentic success should be celebrated, "Make it meaningful. Give honor where honor is due. Make them feel like they're respected in a certain way. If the kid feels like they're receiving attention, like they're receiving love, like they're receiving respect. Like they're — whatever they're after — if they're getting that from this task they're going to keep doing it."

Discussions about goal setting can also help kids gain a better handle on reality and set them up for success in the future. Author Mark LaMaster penned a book with step-by-step guidance to help fathers connect with their sons on a deeper level.

One of his favorite "game days" in the book deals with an issue that many kids and parents struggle with: developing true contentment rather than a sense of entitlement. As part of the "pre-game" preparation, Mark uses a story from his own teen years describing how his basketball team made do with old uniforms and less than ideal circumstances, yet worked hard enough to elbow out a team that had the "coolest" uniforms available (complete with tear-away pants). Telling a story his son can relate to is part of his effort to help illustrate the concept of being content in any situation as described by the Apostle Paul in the Bible.

The "game" gets into the fun for a 10-year-old boy — a chance to pick out his "dream car" and take it for a test drive. Thanks to help from a car dealership owner, Mark was able to take his son out in a Corvette — then dad picked out the second car they drove, "It's the worst, the ugliest, the rustiest car in the lot." Mark says, "And the point is that they both get you from point A to point B and you're not entitled have a Corvette right when you get done with school. It's something you need to work towards and that the purpose of the vehicle is to get you from point A to point B. It's not to impress other people and you should be content and thankful that you have a car because there's people all around the world who don't have cars."

Mark says that practical — and fun — object lesson provides the perfect springboard in the "post-game" interview to start talking about the material things in our lives, "We just started talking about some of the things that we have at our house and he started thinking about how the stuff that he has versus some of his friends have and he says, 'Oh that's why he might think that.'" He says, "We just started digging deeper. We started asking more questions and kind of went off script. This game plan is not to be followed step-by-step. My hope is it will go even somewhere else dads don't even expect it to go; but we had fun driving the car. He thought it was cool and told his friends the next day." Most importantly he says, "We shared that moment... he knows what the Bible says about contentment now and he understands the word entitlement and that he shouldn't just expect to have everything spoon fed to him."

That kind of thoughtful and intentional teaching can also help kids understand that achieving their expectations and dreams for life will require some serious planning, goal setting, and plenty of hard work. It can also encourage them to make sure the dreams they're chasing and goals they are setting are truly worthwhile.

Goal Setting Success

Homeschool alumna Crystal Paine turned a passion for staying out of debt into a highly successful business. The moneysavingmom.com founder shared her frugal tips and encouragement with her readers. In time, website affiliate fees and advertising helped her and her husband, Jesse, purchase their first home with cash.[48]

Since then their business has only continued to expand with Crystal accepting speaking invitations all over the country, landing book contracts, and launching product lines.

While Crystal never attended college to learn about business, she's clearly committed to life-long learning, regularly reading a wide variety of books and sharing what she found most helpful with her blog readers.

Crystal also credits her mom with starting her on the right path with practical lessons in home management before she ever left home. A coupon organization box, book teaching about frugal home management, along with the opportunity to shop, menu-plan, and cook for her parents and six siblings gave Crystal a solid foundation on which to build her home and business.[49]

Today Crystal is also working to help other women experience the same kind of success through her blogging, speaking, and book entitled *Money-Making Mom*. She and her husband are also busy raising their three children.

PROFILE
Bridget Woodman: Supporting Self-Directed Learning

The first day I met six-year-old Alana I immediately knew she was different than many of her peers. In a culture where even preschoolers face an incredible amount of pressure to perform at high levels, she is the most truly accomplished young child I have met and is incredibly hungry to learn more. She also evidently enjoys the process.

The daughter of a Taiwanese mother and German father (who is also an American citizen), she is fluent in English, German, and Chinese. Her parents intentionally spoke to her in each language in shifts to ensure she would learn naturally and easily. In the process, they also gave her an apparent love of language. She is now studying Japanese and Spanish. All this and she has never enrolled in a formal school in a country where early formal education is a universal expectation.

Her mother, Bridget, says the decision to keep her out of preschool was motivated by a desire to help her daughter to learn multiple languages and yet maintain her own interests, "We want our daughter to be a self-motivated learner and not only listen to the teachers' orders. She has freedom to decide what to learn and what to read every day." According to Bridget, Taiwan preschools tend to place too much pressure on young children to write and little emphasis on critical thinking exercises.

Of course, in a country where Alana's education is a radical deviation from the norm, many friends have questioned her mother's approach. Bridget has heard concerns that her daughter won't be able to catch up with the country's school schedule or that she doesn't have a normal social life with kids the same age, but Bridget says she's at peace with her chosen approach. "I don't feel pressure because the decision is made by both my husband and me. We both have agreed that Taiwanese schools are way too... concentrated on test and grades." She says that results in kids who can't think about things that truly interest them, "Most of them lose the passion of learning and creativity."

Instead, Bridget has become an active part of the small Taiwanese homeschooling community, "I started creating learning groups for my daughter, so she has friends to learn together." She has also applied to officially homeschool her daughter — an extensive process requiring curriculum review — and received approval from the education bureau.

Today, Alana is using the extra time and flexibility offered by homeschooling to chase some of her own dreams. Bridget says early on, she and her husband learned a lot about their daughter by reading plenty of storybooks and letting her paint. In the process, they started to notice what she likes, is good at, and what makes her happy. From an early age they provided her with art tools and took her to visit an art teacher. They also noticed that when music is on she enjoys dancing and moving her body.

Then, one day when she was five years old, Alana said, "Mommy, I want to learn skating." Bridget started learning as much as she could about ice skating, took Alana to watch skaters, and allowed her to start learning by hiring a coach to teach inline skating in a local park. Alana now has also learned to ice skate — despite the limited facilities available locally. Today, the mother and daughter travel to Taiwan's capital city for Alana to learn figure skating from an International Skating Union coach — and take part in competitions.

Bridget says, "I know that we are going to spend lots of time and money to support her interests, but I'd like to give my daughter an opportunity to see the world and achieve her dream."

REVIEW
Steps to Inspire Your Children

1. Protect their time: Children need time to explore their world and learn to become quietly comfortable with themselves.

2. Set Expectations: Children need to know that their parents expect them to do well and to get opportunities to prove it.

3. Let Them Dream: Inspiration is an essential component in the learning process — so let children explore topics that fascinate them.

4. Teach Goal Setting: Children need to experience the process of planning and achieving things that just seem "too big" to accomplish.

STEP 5: WORK SMART

"We'd never think of buying the same size of shoes for all six-year-olds! No, we take a child to have his feet measured and see what fits. In the same way, we try to fit the program to where the child is developmentally and experientially within the limits inherent in different teaching situations."

Susan Schaeffer Macaulay, When Children Love to Learn

J oyce Swann saw every one of her children graduate from college by age 15. They worked year round for three hours each morning. This mother of 10 credits part of that success to keeping her kids on-track, never cutting corners, and yet finding the most efficient ways to work.[50]

No matter your curriculum approach or schedule, learning to identify potential time wasters and creating efficient systems is a skill that will benefit your kids long after their school days are over.

When it comes to teaching kids, I prioritize three key concepts: focused work, relevant content, and targeting strengths and weaknesses.

First, I want to clarify what I mean when I use those terms — then we will walk through an example of practical application.

Focused

The opportunity to hyper-focus is one of the greatest strengths afforded by homeschooling. Even in a busy household it is possible to create an environment where a child is doing highly productive "deep work." One way to accomplish this is by focusing most effort on a key subject area while other academic areas are merely in "maintenance mode."

For instance, my daughter may maintain her progress in math and handwriting each day by completing a lesson in each daily. Her daily work is reinforcing concepts already introduced. Meanwhile, she's focused on mastering new material in her English Grammar workbook. Since she isn't splitting her time with other subjects, she can dig deep in this one area moving quickly through lessons she easily grasps then slowing down to internalize more difficult concepts.

Once she masters this area then our primary focus will shift to another subject. Possibly Zoology or Composition. It's good to incorporate numerous academic subjects to keep student interest high, but if covering it all becomes difficult it's a good idea to consider whether the student's attention is becoming fragmented. Many times allowing a child to really dive deep into a specific subject will boost confidence as it's encouraging to see real progress being made.

Relevant

I will never forget tutoring a sweet, bright, artistic young girl about to enter the fifth grade — and still unable to read. At first I was puzzled. She understood the basics of phonics and she wasn't particularly difficult or set against learning to read. She didn't seem to be dyslexic. She didn't even dislike books — she told me about some books read in her class about kids just like those in her school. After a bit of prodding, I realized she simply didn't expect to learn anything new — anything that would stir her artistic heart — inside a book. A historical fiction book soon solved that problem. Calico fabric and kerosene lanterns sparked her imagination and within weeks she was not only reading, but eager to start the next book. It was hard work, but the transformation was rapid once she caught a vision for reading.

So, when I refer to relevancy I'm not suggesting that curriculum merely references what a child already knows. This is a dynamic process of broadening a child's horizons by sparking the imagination and then circling back to plant specific academic skills in that fertile ground.

Targeted

Another huge advantage of homeschooling is that, unlike a teacher with 20 or 30 students in a class, you only need to teach this one student. I am so thankful for the excellent curriculum options available and yet there are workbooks I simply don't use and other resources I've purchased which some families would likely find unnecessary.

For instance, I typically skip using reading comprehension guides because my kids naturally analyze books in-depth — asking questions when they don't understand part of the storyline or asking about words they don't recognize. There is absolutely no sense in turning what they love to do into a drudgery by filling their days with paperwork. Instead, I let them fully enjoy the literature and provide other material to practice handwriting. On the other hand, I found that my daughter does require in-depth spelling instruction. So, the money that would have been spent on reading comprehension materials is instead directed toward a high-quality spelling curriculum.

Practical Application

We can now look at how these components come into play in several stages as we plan to teach the most foundational academic skill: reading.

Pre-Reading (Stage One)

Focused work: At this stage, my efforts center on the one thing proven to develop reading readiness — reading aloud. I can still incorporate in the sensory-rich experiences kids need at this time by letting them play with modeling mediums such as Play-Doh, or my favorite, Smooshi, while I'm reading aloud. They may also color, draw, pretend to write, and cut with scissors. But my effort is focused on making sure I create an environment where they learn to love books.

This also means I'm making sure to control other factors that could reduce their interest in books, such as television and tablet games. While some families totally or nearly eliminate digital media from their homes, we do allow our children to watch some videos and use tablets. However, we are careful to limit the time and curate the content. Most importantly, we watch to make sure they don't develop a glazed-over look, indicating that they've shut off their brains and are just seeing colors and movement. We make sure the focus of their young lives doesn't become a favorite television program — good books continue to capture their imaginations.

Relevant: Starting out, some of the best books mix the familiar with fanciful storylines. When wrapped up in gorgeous illustrations they capture young imaginations. Over time, you can progress to slowly reading chapter books with few pictures. Start out by reading for five minutes at a time. You may be surprised by how soon they will enjoy this. I remember my oldest son coming to me before he was two years old requesting that I read "House the Prairie" (Little House on the Prairie).

That said, this isn't a competition to get your toddler to listen to the thickest books possible. The most important thing to establish at this point is a love for books. That will make it a lot easier to convince your child that it will be worth it to go through the hard work of learning to read.

Targeted: This is a fun part of the process at a time when your child's personality is both forming and being revealed.

Taking turns picking books to read is a great way to learn about your child's interests while still presenting unfamiliar material. In time you will be able to select new books that will delight your little one. Visit tericapshaw.com for a list of our favorite books.

Early Phonics Instruction (Stage Two)

Focused work: When introducing phonics to my children, I limit formal instruction to just 15 minutes a day. That can seem like a long time for a little person, but the amazing part is how much information they can soak up and retain when you keep lessons short and simple. That small block of instructional time in days filled with imaginative play and a few read-aloud stories can be just as effective — and often-times far more effective — than an elite, intensive pre-K or Kindergarten program.

Relevant: Creating a world where reading is a fun and exciting concept is so important at this point. After all, learning to read is incredibly intense work. This is one area where I leverage the magnetic-like draw of videos.

Preschool Press, Rock N' Learn, Super Why, and LeapFrog videos all teach phonics — and the last two do it through compelling storylines many kids love.

The LeapFrog Letter Factory and related videos are especially helpful. In fact, my first two readers were able to completely skip over the entire section of their phonics books covering basic letter sounds. Interestingly, this may be because that video series uses a story-telling method to teach phonics.

Targeted: Many schools and curriculums are designed to teach reading through writing. However, that's not how all kids are wired. Some kids do learn reading best by repeating phonetic sounds while writing, but many others are frustrated by the process of writing while they're trying to learn to read. Although it was challenging (in a good way) at the time, my oldest daughter is clearly a natural at reading. She learned rapidly and was reading at a fourth-grade level when she was five years old. However, she found handwriting difficult and simply wasn't ready to write as early as she was ready to read. In the next year, she also learned to write well. If she had been forced to complete a workbook page for each phonics lesson she would have certainly missed reading hundreds of books in the time that passed between when she was ready to read and when she was ready to write — and the process would have been a lot more frustrating for both of us.

Developing Fluency (Stage Three)

Focused work: At this point, the child knows how to sound out words using phonetic rules, however the process is slow and choppy. Continuing with 15-minute lessons each day, I read aloud with the child occasionally pausing and letting the child sound out the word on his or her own to make sure the child is still reading along rather than just repeating what I'm saying.

Relevant: Simple books with words the child can successfully read that progress in complexity gradually are so helpful at this point. Kids need so much encouragement during this part of the process to make sure they aren't overwhelmed by the complexity of English. Phonetic readers that also capture a child's interest are wonderful. The readers for the All About Reading program are some of the best I've seen. But these days there are many wonderful options for reading books on the market — you're sure to find something that will suit your child's taste.

It's also great to read more difficult books with your children by having them read all the simple words in a story while you read the more complex words. It allows kids to see how much they've already learned and how much more there is to master.

Targeted: This is a good time to put together a shelf or basket of appealing books the child can now read or almost read. Some kids will be bragging to everyone who will listen about their new skills while others prefer to quietly perfect their technique.

Reading Comprehension and Vocabulary Building (Stage Four)

Focused work: At this point, your child is reading independently. If you have an enthusiastic reader it may be tempting to consider reading instruction finished. However, I recommend selecting a few challenging titles to have your child read aloud each year. Some studies have shown that early readers are prone to fall behind children who learned to read later in life. This is likely due to their inability to decode and understand vocabulary words in higher grades.

Relevant: This is a fun time when you can provide books likely to appeal to your child's interest. You can also find stories to help cultivate interest in areas important for your child's academic development. For instance, my daughter absolutely loves a series of math, science, and English books called "Life of Fred." This outlandish character presents some notoriously dry topics in a humorous way that has my daughter hooked.

Targeted: This is a good time to take stock of your child's strengths and weaknesses. Then consider how you can provide opportunities for your child to continue to be challenged in areas where he or she is already strong. In weak areas, prioritize what you want to work on first and tackle each challenge one at a time. This is another area where 15 minutes worth of work per day can make a huge difference.

HARD WORK REWARDED

When Grace Bush graduated from college a week before graduating from high school in 2014, the 16 year old told a TODAY.com reporter that it wasn't hard — just "hard work."[51] The Florida teen managed to complete high school, earn a bachelor's degree in criminal justice, and play the flute in two orchestras simultaneously.

Grace, one of nine children in her family, was homeschooled until she was 13 years old — and eventually joined her two older sisters at Florida Atlantic University High School. The school offers students a chance to earn bachelor's degrees while completing their high school work. Best of all, all three sisters managed to earn their bachelor's degrees without spending any money on tuition.

PROFILE
Dave Gross: Focusing on Quality and Character

Dave Gross and his wife decided to keep their three kids at home before homeschooling was a common practice in Ohio, "We did not call ours homeschooling. We called ours home educating because we weren't interested in taking school home. We were interested in educating our kids in things that were eternal."

Dave, a pastor, says he's noticed that many times parents want their kids to have everything better than they did — and to be better than they were. He says there's a danger that some parents will, "Actually take that and they transfer their own life expectations onto their kids and they try to make their kids be something... that their kids aren't designed to be."

The perspective that God created children with their own DNA and "their own bend" was something he and his wife kept in mind as they set out with a goal to not develop "smart kids", but rather to "make kids of quality and character."

That meant his two sons and one daughter spent as little time as possible doing formal academics — so they could move on to hands-on learning projects on the three acres of land they called home. Dave says, "I'd say 'Grab the hammers and grab the saws and the tape measuring and we'll go out in the backyard." Before long the kids would learn how to use those tools in the process of building a tree house.

The family also took advantage of added flexibility to travel — camping all over the United States and taking the kids along for pastors' conferences. The return flight from one such trip provided an unexpected opportunity to show how an education focused on character also produced excellent academic results.

"There was a man on the aisle seat, then our son, and then I was against the window. My son and I we were doing some of his math. This guy about broke his neck watching what we were doing and finally he said, 'How old is your son?' I said he's 5 or 6 or something like that. He said, 'That Math he's doing 2nd or 3rd grade math.'" It turned out that the man was actually a guidance counselor for the family's local school district.

Sometime after that, Dave and his wife sent a letter informing the city that they planned to home educate. The school district officials responded by asking about their curriculum and requesting a meeting. (This was before the state of Ohio had a homeschooling provision.)

Dave remembers the day of the meeting well, "We went in and they said, 'Why do you want to do this?'" He continues, "Well, I just took my Bible and flopped it down and said, 'You know Malachi chapter 4 verse 6 says the fathers shall train up their children and to have hearts after them.'" He was explaining that educating his kids was a personal religious conviction — and that he was going to do it — when, "in walks this guy that had been on the airplane and he was actually like a testimony or a witness for us saying, 'I don't think you need to worry about these people giving these kids an education because their [son] is already doing math a couple years ahead.'"

It turns out that the guidance counselor was right. Each year, the Gross kids would take a standardized test and invariably Dave says they would score in the 95th to 98th percentile in all subjects. But he ads that, "It wasn't because we were pushing them. We just went along at their pace and we didn't want them working hour after hour at home. We just wanted them to put in a good amount of time and that was the result of just doing it."

Dave says that trying to make education fun paid off when their oldest son took the GED test — he got a scholarship based on his score. He ended up getting a master's degree from Missouri State University and went on to take the military linguistics exam with a score only a couple of points off the highest grade on record. The other two kids have also launched successful careers close to home as their second son is the youth pastor in their church and their daughter manages a highly profitable daycare for the church.

Dave's advice for parents just starting out in this journey? Focus on character education and don't worry about the details, "People get all knotted up over their kids have to get these grades and perform or they're going to be failures. Parents' expectations are probably one of the most dangerous things for raising good kids."

Dave and Kay Gross founded Radiant Life Church in Dublin, Ohio.

REVIEW
Steps to Inspire Your Children

1. Protect their time: Children need time to explore their world and learn to become quietly comfortable with themselves.

2. Set Expectations: Children need to know that their parents expect them to do well and to get opportunities to prove it.

3. Let Them Dream: Inspiration is an essential component in the learning process — so let children explore topics that fascinate them.

4. Teach Goal Setting: Children need to experience the process of planning and achieving things that just seem "too big" to accomplish.

5. Work Smart: Children can accomplish amazing things when we value their time and help them learn to use it well.

Step 6: Encourage Independent Work

"Rather than just being equipped for advanced learning, children need to become competent life-long learners; this way, they won't end up with merely a paper degree, coupled with insurmountable debt, only later to discover that what they've learned will not automatically guarantee them future success in life."

Sherry K. Hayes, *Homeschool Sanity*

Teaching kids to take personal responsibility for their work at a young age is often essential in homeschool households with many children learning at various grade levels. But it also benefits children in any size family or schooling situation.

There's a sense of pride and self-respect children experience as they learn to properly manage their own workloads. In fact, learning to work independently is something Paul and Tori Fish make sure they intentionally teach each child. Tori says, "For us one of our biggest goals in the overall academic realm is teaching our children how to learn and if they can learn on their own they can do about anything that they want to do."

In their family, it's part of a gradual process of first teaching young kids to focus on the work at hand then helping them grow more responsible as the years pass.

"In the very young, young years if we've made the schedule, we have them stick to it but as they get older and older, you know, they have a little bit of input and there's a lot less oversight." Paul says that around seventh or eighth grade, "We start to give them a little bit of rope. Not enough to hang themselves on but probably enough to trip them up. And Algebra 1 seems to be one of those places." In their family, sometimes a child has to repeat Algebra 1, but Paul says it's a valuable life lesson.

Bradley Fish says that his parents' approach helped him finish school and launch a career in record time, "It taught me how to teach myself and both when I was working through college, and trying to get that done very quickly, as well as when I got into the business world and I had to learn new computer programs or learn a new field of business and try to do it on the fly to my boss's satisfaction."

Bradley says learning to teach himself as a teen helped him learn to identify what he needed to know to master a concept — and understand his own learning style, "Those were very helpful things that I got from homeschooling and part of that is I had the flexibility. I got to try different types of learning."

But Bradley says a solid foundation provided by his parents was even more important than the freedom to work independently, "I got a really good worldview and it was consistent. Obviously, the same teachers all the way through. So I didn't have to deal with conflicting perspectives or world views as I grew up and that gave me a really strong foundation and something that I've been able to base all the rest of my life on."

Teacher Michael Myers says parents who send their kids to school can also have a positive impact by encouraging kids to solve problems and accomplish their own goals. That may involve helping kids identify the tools they can use such as looking something up in a book, reading articles, or search-ing for YouTube videos. The goal is to create habits to feed inquisitive minds as children grow, "I think they continue that learning lifestyle that is instilled in us from birth."

Nurturing that type of learning can also involve choosing the best way to respond to questions that naturally pop up during a day. Michael says, "When you answer [kids' ques-tions] right off the bat, you're really robbing them of a chance to go on this journey to figure out something on their own." Instead he insists that whenever a child asks a question he or she gets, "sent on a quest."

"When a kid asks me a question I say, 'How quickly does the kid need the answer?' There are different ways. 'Should I give the answer now or later?'" Michael says he also considers the learning opportunity at hand, "'Are there things that he or she could pick up on this quest, on this journey to the answer, that are necessary for thinking skills?' And if there are I will ask another question."

Of course, it all depends upon how serious the child is about the question — the key it to make sure to provide plenty of opportunities for children to think for themselves and organize their thoughts in a meaningful way.

Michael says great teachers can also bring this type of learning into a classroom setting, "These teachers that are experienced in this stuff, have a way of making room for the kids' desires and learning isn't about mastering these facts. Learning is about teaching kids how to organize facts and to search for facts that they need to get a certain outcome."

That approach takes the focus off of mere content and on to the more important art of managing the overload of information available in our world, "It's more about trying to master a way to present the content — how to organize the content. So you have kids giving a how to speech or giving more information about popcorn, about how to fix a radiator or something else."

Independent or "child interest led" learning can be directed by a parent or teacher. Something Michael says that can still be done in a way that encourages the child, "There are still times where you have to learn a certain thing so you can help them apply the skills from their interest learning to what they have to learn about. And then celebrate their victories and praise them for it and let them know what they're doing well specifically. And also let them know how they can improve specifically."

Bradley says he's thankful that his parents intentionally allowed him to learn how to work independently while completing assigned work, "I won't say that I learned time management quickly or perfectly but it was something where I did realize, 'Ok, at the end of the year I have to have this done.'" And he says that helped him learn to take action, "And as a habitual procrastinator through the younger grades I did realize finally, 'Ok, I have to buckle down and finish this.'"

PRETEEN COLLEGE STUDENTS

When she was four years old Hannah Harding's dad entertained himself by teaching her trigonometry tricks as he worked on his own college homework.[52] At that time, Kip and Mona Lisa Harding probably never imagined that they would ultimately have 10 children.

In their book, *The Brainy Bunch* the Hardings tell how each child started taking college classes by 12 years old (some even as young as 10). Now the family has an engineer, architect, and one of America's youngest doctors. The younger siblings include an entrepreneur, composer, aspiring professor, and a 10-year-old set to become a lawyer.

Mona Lisa Harding says her younger children all started college by 12 because it's normal in their family. All of the kids seem to pick up on family expectations whether they were intentionally created or not.

AN INVENTOR'S DREAM SCHOOL

"Ad Astra", Latin for "to the stars" is an exclusive school housed in a mansion with just 20 students and three teachers. The student roster includes billionaire Elon Musk's five sons. In an interview with Bejing TV, the inventor explained that traditional schools, "weren't doing the things I thought should be done."[53] So, he decided to create his own school which offers students an opportunity to learn specific skill sets rather than following traditional grade structures.

Musk says a focus on problem solving is much better than the traditional approach of teaching about tools needed to accomplish a task. For instance, the Tesla founder says an the most effective way to teach about engines is hands-on and instantly meaningful, "Here's the engine. Now let's take it apart. How are we gonna take it apart? Oh you need a screwdriver."[54]

COLLEGE WORK INITIATIVE

Learning to work independently may be the single greatest strength most homeschool students bring to the table when applying for college. Often ranked as the number one university in the world, MIT is one of the elite schools happy to accept applications from homeschooled students.

Less than 1% of all applicants (and of the student body) come from a homeschooling background, but the admissions office provides some tips on its website for those students:

> *"One quality that we look for in all of our applicants is evidence of having taken initiative, showing an entrepreneurial spirit, taking full advantage of opportunities. Many of our admitted homeschooled applicants have really shined in this area. These students truly take advantage of their less constrained educational environment to take on exciting projects,*

go in depth in topics that excite them, create new opportunities for themselves and others, and more."[55]

For a link to the rest of MIT's admission tips and more information about college planning visit www.tericapshaw.com/dyingtowin.

PART 2 REVIEW
Steps to Inspire Your Children to Learn

1. Protect their time: Children need time to explore their world and learn to become quietly comfortable with themselves.

2. Set Expectations: Children need to know that their parents expect them to do well and to get opportunities to prove it.

3. Let Them Dream: Inspiration is an essential component in the learning process — so let children explore topics that fascinate them.

4. Teach Goal Setting: Children need to experience the process of planning and achieving things that just seem "too big" to accomplish.

5. Work Smart: Children can accomplish amazing things when we value their time and help them learn to use it well.

6. Encourage Independent Work: Taking responsibility for their own learning is a skill that will help children in the future as much as any academic subject they may study.

STEP 7: PRACTICE CONTENTMENT

"An inheritance is what you leave people.
A legacy is what you leave in them."

Craig D. Lounsbrough

"So, this thing that looks like a bee carrying a bag of garbage," Eliana brushed some hair out of her eyes, "is really 'of.'"

She had learned to write cursive letters and had moved on to copying Bible verses for practice. And she sure needed that practice.

This is where my judgment as a parent is most needed — and most critical. I need to allow my children to reach their full potential, but I also need to know when to acknowledge, "Yes, that word does look more like a housecleaning insect than either of us intended, but it's good enough for today."

I grew up with the modern homeschool movement and watched some families thrive while others, who seemed to "have it all together," floundered during their children's teen years. That experience has led me to believe that knowing what is good enough (or just *enough*, for that matter) and keeping all achievement in perspective is the key to creating a peaceful household and raising kids who are secure in their abilities, yet not arrogant.

This is one concept the parents and experts I've talked to all identify as a key component to successful parenting and educating in a stressful age. It's perhaps one of the most difficult things to do, but as a society and as individual parents it's time to "lighten up."

Teacher and reading coach Michael Myers also says it's time to take a deep look at our motives and ask ourselves why we're pushing so hard for kids to be successful. If we can't find a "noble reason" it's time to adjust our actions to make sure they really align with our values and belief systems.

Paul and Tori Fish say that over the years, their approach to educating their children has matured with a greater focus on core values, "When we look at our journey of why we homeschooled I would say it's changed over time." Paul says, "Early on, our attitude was a little bit more of 'we can do it better, faster, and cheaper than a private school or public school." But these days — especially as their children have gotten older — Paul says, "Homeschooling has become much more of 'How do we train our children?' And academics has been secondary."

Of course, it's easy to ponder what *really* matters during quiet reflection, but what about when you start chatting with other parents? Paul says that is when a parent's commitment to contentment is most challenged, "Of course, in that conversation it feels like everybody else's children are light years ahead of yours. And they're all doing these fantastic things. And all we're doing is just kind of sitting at home living life is what it feels like."

He says although pressure to perform is always a factor, homeschooling does minimize constant comparison, "It offers you the opportunity to pull out of, or disengage, not from society, but from the compelling need or feeling that you have to compete with everybody else."

At the same time, the sheer amount of responsibility homeschooling represents also poses its own challenges. Erica McCuen says fear is a major stress factor, "So many moms going through it think 'I'm not doing it right.'" And there's nothing like a good homeschooling conference, full of fantastic resources, to make parents question whether their current course is really best. Yet Erica says staying on track with a particular curriculum that's working for your students is key, but the temptation to adopt the latest great system is "so tormenting." Ultimately, she says every successful school year decision comes down to relying on her core values and beliefs, "Mainly trusting God that's how I got through. Just trusting Him with everything."

Nervousness and performance anxiety doesn't just haunt homeschool parents. As a teacher and parent, Michael knows its a universal challenge, "Parents need to, myself included, think 'How would I feel if my son was delayed in a certain way?' There's a temptation to feel like I've let my son down. I didn't do the right things as a parent, but it's not always my fault. You know, sometimes it's just the way he's developing."

Balancing a healthy level of ambition with a soul-nourishing level of contentment is not only healthy for our families — it's also something our growing children desperately need someone to model for them. Paul says a certain amount of competitiveness within the family can be a good thing, "But there also needs to be a contentment amongst your children about how they're gifted and what they're good at." He says that can also provide opportunities to develop healthy relationships and develop character, "If one child excels at a particular subject, you know, that's his or her opportunity to help his brothers or sisters in a way that his brothers or sisters actually want to be helped. And not, maybe, lord it over them."

But perhaps the best piece of advice to cultivate true contentment comes from William Estrada, a homeschool advocate and former student: enjoy teaching your children. "I always remind parents, 'Make the education fun.'" He says, "The love of learning is one of the most amazing, I believe God-given things that human beings have." He adds, "Channel that creative energy — that love of learning — and you'll be creating something wonderful that your children will take with them their entire lives."

WINNING DAD PLAYS

Author Mark LaMaster says he's just another dad, "I'm not an expert. I'm not a perfect dad — I still have lots of questions — but I'm trying and I want other dads to try." He says kids will notice that effort — even if the initial attempts to connect feel a bit awkward, "I think we can help get God's message out there and will become closer to our sons either way. If we embarrass ourselves that might be even better than anything else that we do."

Mark's effort to connect on a deep level with his 10-year-old son Lincoln is not only impressive– it's paving the way for other dads to do the same. He collaborated with his son to create a road map for fathers to follow in his book *Friday Night Lights for Fathers and Sons: Schedule a 10-Game Winning Season to help develop your son into the man God intended him to be.*[56]

Each of the ten "game days" are structured to help fathers and sons spend quality time together creating fun memories– and prompt conversations that will help them build an even stronger relationship.

Mark also plans to build a Facebook community for like-minded fathers. He says he, like many guys, needs to work on his male friendships, "We don't talk about, 'So what kind of things are you doing to really get to know your son better?'" He says, "It's kind of weird we don't want to admit that we're struggling with it so I want to create a community like that to give them some tools and also give them a community to bounce ideas off of each other I'm looking forward to learning from it too."

REVIEW
Steps to Inspire Your Children

1. Protect their time: Children need time to explore their world and learn to become quietly comfortable with themselves.

2. Set Expectations: Children need to know that their parents expect them to do well and to get opportunities to prove it.

3. Let Them Dream: Inspiration is an essential component in the learning process — so let children explore topics that fascinate them.

4. Teach Goal Setting: Children need to experience the process of planning and achieving things that just seem "too big" to accomplish.

5. Work Smart: Children can accomplish amazing things when we value their time and help them learn to use it well.

6. Encourage Independent Work: Taking responsibility for their own learning is a skill that will help children in the future as much as any academic subject they may study.

7. Practice Contentment: Parents and children both need a good grasp on their core values so they will know when what they have accomplished is "good enough."

PART 3

BREAKING FREE: BUILD AN EDUCATIONAL LEGACY

TRUE FREEDOM

"Children are born persons."

Charlotte Mason

This section is where we get real about what the stories in this book have to do with you and your child. I want to provide some great resources and solid practical advice regarding ways you can help your child achieve his or her full potential. But first, it's time for a reality check.

We have good reason to be outraged by an education system poised to push, prod, and mold our children into products that will improve the system's standing on the world stage. However, it's critical to ensure that we don't recreate the same kind of situation at home.

The time and dedication you are willing to pour into your child is apparent simply because you've made it to this chapter — and that's a great thing! But here's a tough question: Are you willing to pour your life into making sure your child gets the best education possible and then let that child go on to make his or her own life choices as an adult? Or are you subconsciously mapping out your child's perfect life through retirement? These are not questions to put off until high school graduation. The answer will provide insight into whether you are truly preparing your child for his or her future — or setting yourself up for disappointment.

In the prologue to her book, *Mere Motherhood*, Cindy Rollins reflects on her own journey as a homeschool mother to her nine children, "One of the biggest dangers homeschooling moms face is letting their relationships (with their children) become idols of the heart." She writes, "It is easy for this idolatry to lay dormant and festering for years, undiscovered, causing damage."[57]

As a child, I noticed a few homeschool families crafting what looked like unrealistically perfect childhoods and educations for their children. I was always thankful that my mother took a far more relaxed approach. As a teen and young adult, I often imagined those parents collectively gasping when their children started going against their parents' dearest ideals — sometimes overcompensating I'm sure — as they started directing their own lives.

Now, this is in no way an argument against homeschooling — or in taking a deep interest in your child's education in other ways — but rather an effort to think deeply and more clearly about our roles and goals as parents. It's easy to let things become complicated, but what our children need most is simply the opportunity to develop into the unique people they were born to become. And it seems parents stand to learn and grow more than we ever expected in the process. We're challenged to strike a balance between providing enough oversight to make sure our children are started on the right path and making sure that we don't let our parental ideals get in the way.

In fact, as our children's first teachers — which we all are — a parent's single greatest contribution may be simply leading the way by showing our children how to become life-long learners. In the process, I believe you can become your child's greatest teacher because I experienced this myself.

My mother struggled in school but she's dedicated to lifelong learning and gave me an amazing K-12 homeschool education. She loves to tell how she finally learned to sound out long words that had always baffled her as she studied the teacher's materials for my kindergarten phonics program. (Imagine my shock when I got the same program for my own daughter and discovered that my mom had read more than 500 pages preparing for that epic task.)

While it isn't mandatory to take teacher prep to that extreme, choosing to teach your children at home is a major commitment that can try any parent's patience. As an experienced homeschooler with ten kids, Tori Fish knows all about the ups and downs of educating at home.

"It's a journey." She says, "It's a process. It's day-by-day. Sometimes you feel like that was a great few hours of school there and other times you feel like you just took several steps backward." Taking those bumps in the road in stride is key, "A lot of people think, 'Oh, you just must be amazing to do what you do, but really we're not." Tori says, "We get frustrated and have to step back and say 'Ok, what are we trying to accomplish here? What are our goals? And what are we doing based on our goals?"

Exactly what those goals are — and how you can and will impact your child's future — is well worth pondering as we explore several aspects of homeschooling in this section. But first we'll take a look at how you can incorporate some of the concepts presented in this book right away — even if your child is already in a traditional school setting.

CHAPTER REVIEW

What our children need most is the opportunity to develop into the unique people they were born to become. We can help by giving them opportunities to become life-long learners.

A JUMPSTART

"A human being is meant to be taught by human beings for human things. That can never be accomplished be mere methods."

*Anthony Esolen, Life Under Compulsion:
Ten Ways to Destroy the Humanity of Your Child*

"Remember how you never brought home homework as a kid?" My husband gave a vague answer that meant he might or might not actually be listening to me. (I totally do this too — he's caught me.) I persisted, "Do you know why?"

"Because it was easier to do it then and because I wanted to enjoy my evening." He responded.

"And when does your mom do the supper dishes?" I quizzed.

"Right away. Because it's easier and because she wants to enjoy her evening."

Of course, this conversation took place as the supper bowls from our meal developed crusty dried-on food residue. But let's not talk about that. The point is that my mother-in-law is awesome. And that my husband's parents strongly influenced their three children who all attended public school.

You won't have the same level of authority as you would if exclusively homeschooling — kids answer to their teachers for most of the day. But I believe you can use the seven steps suggested in the last section to influence your children.

According to educator Michael Myers, it's critical for parents and teachers to be, "on the same team, pushing the same way." Unlike homeschooling where parents chart a course for their children and adjust as needed, parents with students in a traditional school setting need to carefully consider what their children are mentally processing from their time in the classroom.

"It's very important to be on the same page with the teacher. You don't want these competing problem-solving skills because our brain likes to be as efficient and use as little energy as possible and the best way to do that is to create an efficient processing system."

Most importantly, parents need to be careful to avoid frustrating their children. Teaching alternative problem-solving techniques can force a child to expend brain power trying to decide which process to follow and can, Michael says, ultimately backfire in the end, "When you instill these competing ways, you're asking your kid to learn more. To work harder. That can instill bitterness in your kid. That can instill anger."

Obviously, this means helping with homework can be tricky. Michael says that you need to have a clear understanding of your role in helping with homework. He says to be sure to communicate with your child's teacher, "Don't try to solve every single problem. I would just ask the teacher, 'What am I expected to do with this assignment? And how can I help my kid solve it?'"

Working on the same team as the teacher means you will not only better understand in what ways your child may be struggling, but also provide opportunities to help him or her finally grasp some elusive concepts.

Another area where parents can help has nothing to do with formal academics, but instead sparking a child's general interest in learning. Michael says after the homework is done, parents can encourage a sense of wonder in their children, "Why not watch a video about fixing cars or playing baseball or something like that? And then show them how to ask good questions about certain things."

In fact, he believes teaching kids to ask great questions is one of the most important things you can do, "Help make your kid a better thinker. An individual, independent thinker. Somebody who can problem solve on [his or her] own."

Of course, at times parents may feel that their children — especially those with special needs — may not be getting enough from their school situation. Michael says there are several ways to advocate for a child in that situation, but he likes to start by equipping kids to make sure their own needs are being met, "Help your child understand what they need and help them to see that, 'This is how I learn. This is how I'm wired. This is what I need to learn. And this is how I can ask for help.'"

Beyond that, he says parents can contact the teacher or district administrators by sending an e-mail, note, making a phone call, or arranging a face-to-face meeting. In some cases, for instance when working with a child with dyslexia, parents may even hire a professional advocate. That advocate can help parents navigate the system and convince a school district to understand that a child has a very different learning style.

That usually involves presenting research to back up any requested changes and basically says, "We want you to teach our kid in a certain way that's research based because what you're doing isn't working."

Once changes are in place, Michael says parents can go back and keep asking the teachers questions, "'How do you think my kid is learning?' 'What obstacles are getting in the way of my kids being where they need to be?'" He says it's also important for parents to fully understand the situation and what type of expectations they should have.

Most important of all, he says, remember to keep encouraging your child to learn to become his or her own advocate, "Ultimately, that's the end goal is to teach a kid how to think so that [he or she] can take care of themselves in today's culture in a way that makes sense."

PROFILE
Michael Myers: Teaching Kids How to Think

As a literacy coach and intervention specialist Michael Myers is familiar with the intense pressure for students to score well in a high performing school district and is well versed in helping "move the needle" on a student's progress.

He started out in his career by teaching at a private Christian school for five years before moving on to work at a top-tier high performing school district in Ohio. Now he works in the special education department helping struggling readers from K-12. He coaches the kids to help them understand the text they are reading, write, and share their ideas. He also has a private business tutoring and building summer plans for reading.

Michael and his wife, Emily, have a two-year-old son, Elliot. He says inspiring his son to think about and question the world we live in is also part of his job as a parent, "I think a big part of learning is learning how to ask good questions and I don't know if learners are being taught how to ask good questions about things. They are kind of taught how to think about something and they kind of run with it but they don't really know how to ask more questions about a certain subject, so if we kind of ask questions yourself to push their learning I think that helps too."

He says you can let others teach your children how to read or do math but, "I think as a parent we're kind of charged with teaching our kids how to think. How to think about content. How to process it."

After all, how we deal with what we learn is a big part of who we are as individuals and members of a family. Michael says, "Coming from a Christian perspective I want my kid to be looking at certain things as through a loving eye, as Christ would a lot of the time. So, there is a lot there that you get a chance to instill family values, family beliefs in learning. And that's the time to give your kid a worldview... not just when you're reading scripture or going to church. You bring up family values during your learning time."

And keeping those family values in mind may just be the key to connecting to something much deeper than mere academics, "I know that with my son Elliot we believe in Christ, we believe in that relationship with Christ and we do think to live life to the full life isn't just about, you know, just getting great grades." Michael says, "It's about perfecting your talents so that you can find fulfillment in helping other people and experiencing that relationship and connection. And so, that's why we go to school and why we do all these things is to build these relationships. And so, I think when kids look at 'I just do this so that I can get a good job, money, and take care of myself... I think a lot of times that doesn't resonate with kids. I think friends and relationships really resonate with kids."

Michael Myers is the founder of Magnifying Talents Tutoring (magnifyingtalents.com). He lives in Ohio with his wife, son, and daughter.

ADVENTURE NANNIES

Some parents may not be ready to homeschool — and yet they have the desire and means to explore the world with their kids. Well, these days there's a service for that.

Adventure Nannies will set families up with their very own private educator. According to the service's website they have educators available with a variety of backgrounds including experienced teachers, homeschool teachers, and tutors. The educators are, "familiar with a variety of progressive educational styles including unschooling, Waldorf, and Montessori, and many are experienced nannies as well."[58]

Visit tericapshaw.com/dyingtowin for more information.

CHAPTER REVIEW

Even if you send your children away to school you still have an important role to play in helping your children develop an active interest in learning and exploring the world.

HOMESCHOOL MEETS THE REAL WORLD

"Will your kids grow up to be weird if you homeschool them? Yes, definitely. Someone — right now, this very minute — thinks you are weird because you are not like them. And someone will think your children are weird for the same reason. But the way you choose to educate them will not be the cause."

Paula Bolyard, Homeschooling: Fighting for My Children's Future

When we first moved to Taiwan many conversations started out like this: "How old is your daughter?" "She's three." I would answer.

"Oh, perfect time to come! Where does she go to school?" My new friend would ask enthusiastically.

"I'm teaching her at home." I would reply.

At this point, the questions would abruptly stop as the poor person would choke on his or her next words in surprise and look a bit unsteady. Inevitably this person would recover enough to extol all the virtues of Taiwan's education system. At some point in that conversation, or in future conversations, the reasonable price of psychiatric care in Taiwan would be brought up.

The point of this story is not to debate the fragility of my mental health. (I do have four children age seven and under.) Rather, I want to point out that doing something different can seem radical in a culture where the schools are considered good. But what if that really good system only works for *most* students and your child — or grandchild — isn't part of that group?

In this chapter, I'm going to outline four reasons often cited as to why homeschooling won't work — and explain why I consider each one as actually an argument in favor of that option.

Socialization

First, let's look at socialization. The concern that homeschooled kids won't get enough social interaction is the single biggest argument I hear against homeschooling. Many people believe that all children need to spend most of their time with kids who are their own age. But arguing that this is true simply because it's common in our current culture doesn't make much sense. It would make just as much sense if you believed fast food is essential for health because most people you know eat it all the time — if that were true you might need a new perspective. In reality, it is good for kids to have opportunities to make friends their own age, but that's not all there is to life. There is value in opportunities to meet and interact with people of all ages and diverse backgrounds.

The opportunity to work directly with a small number of students tends to make homeschooling efficient. Students don't have to move between classes or wait for teachers to help as many other students. This means that they can finish their academic work quickly each day. Then life becomes a field trip. An errand to the bank and grocery store provides real life mathematical story problems and opportunities for kids to observe how to conduct themselves in different settings. There is also time to volunteer with civic organizations and join youth activities. For a list of ideas visit tericapshaw.com/dyingtowin.

It's also important to not assume that simply being with others will result in

positive social development. My husband has wisely pointed out that it is our responsibility as parents, in any academic setting, to ensure that our kids develop the internal character necessary so they will go on to develop healthy relationships with others.

Structure

Homeschooling is something like running your own business — there's tons of flexibility, but you have to be willing to make yourself, and your children, do the work. In fact, you may find that you're not necessarily doing more work as a homeschooling parent — just different work. A friend told me she spent about the same amount of focused, productive time homeschooling her son as she had spent the year before when he was in public school. Why? Before, she spent time getting him and his younger siblings into the car to drop him off and pick him up each day, making sure he completed his homework, attending parent-teacher conferences, and participating in school fundraisers. In short, being a mom is a lot of work no matter how you look at it!

That said, the most effective homeschools are typically tailored to help each child develop life-long learning habits, rather than merely imitate a classroom setting.

Homeschool mom Mystie Winckler says she can see that process happening as her oldest son works through his algebra textbook. He typically prepares to sit down and study by brewing himself a cup of tea. This ritual signals to Mystie that she's on the right path, "This is the pattern that an adult would use if they had work to do or something they wanted to learn," Mystie says, "You'd open a book, get a paper, a pencil, a beverage, and just sit down."

So, what about when it's time to transition to a classroom setting? Personally, I found my first semester in college completely painless. The independent work required in college seems like a natural progression for a student already accustomed to managing his or her own school schedule for many years.

Academic Expertise

This is an area that poses the greatest challenges for homeschooling parents as they enter the high school years. While almost anyone can teach at the elementary level — especially with the excellent curriculum options available today — things can get complicated in the upper grades. Students studying math and science can quickly move past what parents remember from their own high school days. Thankfully, a lot of good options are now available.

Computerized lessons and online classes with live tutors can help. Some parents also join with other parents to pool their knowledge. Many parents also find that they can enroll their teens in community college math classes by the time they've surpassed their parent's abilities and need more than the help offered by a good quality textbook. For a list of resources, including free online classes from some of the most prestigious colleges in the world, visit www.tericapshaw.com/dyingtowin.

In fact, with the rich amount of information readily available today, perhaps the most important factor is not a parent with the right expertise, but one willing to cultivate a contagious interest in all things academic. Whether we're teaching them ourselves or encouraging them in their studies in a traditional school setting, we owe it to our kids to help them develop the tools that will allow them to tackle any endeavor in the future. It's a good idea to make sure that whatever you and your children aren't particularly interested in is scheduled at the top of your homeschool day. After all, no matter how uninspiring it may seem today, solid skills in math, grammar, and writing are likely to be essential building blocks for your child to achieve his or her dreams in the future.

Relationship

The final concern I often hear expressed is one that is more difficult to address. Many parents considering homeschooling say they're not sure they can handle filling the role of parent and teacher. Based on personal experience, I would say there's no difference between being a parent and a teacher. As a parent, you are your child's first teacher and that's a role that never really ends. Where there's a shared love of learning there's always something new to discover in this lifetime.

But I also hear experienced homeschool parents say they had to step back and send their children to school for a time — or wish they had — so they could focus on just being a parent without the stress of also being a teacher.

Ultimately, this is an area where every parent will have to do some serious soul searching. I would simply encourage you to not underestimate the power you may have in your child's life — and consider whether precious time together, perhaps committed to for just one year at a time, may help you build memories you'll treasure for a lifetime.

PROFILE
Mystie Winckler: A Classical Approach at Home

Mystie Winckler and her husband are second generation homeschoolers, yet teaching their own kids at home wasn't plan A. Although they had good homeschooling experiences themselves, Mystie says they were intrigued by a highly successful classical Christian education model, "You had to do all these different things, their approach to classical was very much one that was intimidating to homeschoolers." And the typical homeschool situation where mom is the primary teacher and administrator wasn't encouraged, "There were a lot of voices in that movement that pretty much said, 'Yeah, maybe mom can homeschool the early years but you really need real teachers the older your kids get.'"

Homeschooling remained an option, but one they had a few reservations about. "Being homeschooled we knew that it was wonderful and also [knew] the difficulties as well." Mystie says one concern was whether they would be able to consistently provide all of the educational experiences they wanted their children to have. "When you're at home your best intentions are not generally what happens," She says laughing, "And we were 21 and idealistic."

After Mystie and her husband graduated from college and moved to the Tri-Cities area in Washington state, they spent some time working with a group of people interested in starting a local classical school. "It didn't work out," Mystie says, looking back, "And I'm glad for that."

With no classical school available locally they turned back to the possibility of homeschooling. Mystie started following a blog written by Cindy Rollins which she says opened her eyes to the more liberal arts side of classical education. She was familiar with classical education models that focused on the classical stages of learning called the "Trivium." Now she was discovering so much more beyond the trivium's focus on teaching grammar (memorization), logic, and rhetoric at specific ages. Through an online book club Mystie started reading, "Norms and Nobility: A Treatise on Education" by David Hicks. She says that book provided a vision for what education should be — and what it should not be.

"Our kids aren't ultimately cogs in a machinery for the economy." She says adding that it's important to focus on an education that develops a more well-rounded person rather than focusing solely on college and jobs which, "All basically comes down to money — and that puts, basically, your income potential as the most important characteristic of a person."

Now, with her oldest of five children in middle school, Mystie says she has enjoyed homeschooling with a classical model. In fact, there is now a classical school available in their area, but Mystie and her husband have chosen to continue homeschooling. They enjoy embracing the opportunity to specifically help each child develop as a student and person.

When asked how she teaches her kids compares to her own homeschool experience as a student Mystie says, "I'd say it is a continuation." Back then, she says, classical education wasn't even a conversation point in most homeschool circles, "When I was homeschooled you were pretty much an Abeka or Bob Jones homeschooler."

Mystie's mother assigned Bob Jones workbooks in the mornings and left the afternoons wide-open for reading, "When we said we were doing school that meant our work-books — and we got those done as quickly as we could so that we could do what we actually wanted to do and read."

Mystie's approach with her own kids doesn't involve tests or quizzes, but she does use a math program with a mastery approach. She says that sets a high standard where the students have to completely understand each concept before moving on to the next lesson. She says sometimes that takes two or three weeks or only a couple of days.

According to Mystie the biggest challenge she faces as a homeschool parent is one any parent faces — how to communicate and convince her growing children to accept her authority in her role as a parent.

"I'm kind of right in the middle of middle school right now with my boys and I can see that there's definitely a lot more questioning and trying to push those boundaries and I've seen a lot of parents put their middle school or high school student in school for exactly that reason because they aren't going to treat their teacher the way that they were treating their mom." Mystie says that's something she expects, "Everyone has their public face — when a kid is in school they're putting on that public face and the reason they end up more tired and needing to zone out more when they do have the free time is because that is exhausting to be learning while keeping that public front and kind of filtering everything you're saying and doing through what the teacher is saying, what everyone around you is thinking and doing."

Mystie says homeschooling creates a different kind of dynamic where there is, "No filter and you're seeing what is actually going on in their minds and in their emotions and everything — and so it's exhausting. But it is good to be able to work through that with them." And while that can be difficult to deal with, Mystie says that process may be more important than the academic material being covered. Ultimately, she says homeschooling, "Lets the kids see that they aren't perfect, but it also lets them see that you aren't perfect everyday... and that's a really big deal. How do we as moms fail? And how do we fail in front of them? In all the different kinds of ways? That's the biggest thing that we're modeling when they're with us all the time is: When you mess up what do you do?"

And even though the good years are mixed with many months where she's struggled to work through growing pains with a particular child Mystie says the path they've chosen has been absolutely worth it every step of the way.

Mystie lives in Washington state with her husband and five children. She blogs about homeschooling and organization. Learn more at mystiewinckler.com.

TOO FAR AHEAD FOR SCHOOL

When Jessie Wise decided to teach her two children phonics before they entered school, she had no idea exactly what she was getting herself into. The kids soon needed to move grades ahead to have work at their ability level, but faced teasing from other students due to their young ages. Ultimately, she followed a psychologist's suggestion to just teach them herself.[1] Decades later Jessie and her daughter, Susan Wise Bauer, would share their story in a book called *The Well-Trained Mind* to guide others along the same path. They now have extensive curriculum offerings available through the Peace Hill Press Curriculum company.

CHAPTER REVIEW

While fairly uncommon in today's culture, homeschooling offers unique opportunities for kids to socialize more with people they wouldn't come in contact with in a school setting, learn to structure their days, take advantage of a variety of academic opportunities, and develop deeper relationships with their families.

TRUSTING YOU WITH
YOUR CHILDREN

"So what is the point of school? Long before any teaching takes place, shouldn't we decide what we want to accomplish? Are we merely preparing our children for Jeopardy, or will their education enhance their future lives outside of academia?"

Britton LaTulippe, Revealing School

Choosing to do life differently — no matter how bad the most common path is for your family — always seems to make some people mad. In the 1980s, Iowa homeschool parents were even thrown in jail.[59] But staying true to your own convictions is also rewarding. And these days it's easier than ever to create a support team to help encourage you along your journey to find the best education — and the best life — for your child.

In this chapter, I want to give you resources to learn about legal requirements for homeschooling in your area, find support for homeschooling, and explain your decision to less-than-supportive friends and family.

Laws Governing Homeschooling

Homeschooling is currently legal throughout the entire United States with varying levels of regulation. In several states, parents aren't even required to file a notice of "intent to homeschool" while some require notification, standardized testing, and other requirements such as curriculum approval and visits by state officials. It's important to make sure you thoroughly understand your state's regulations before starting. That way you can make sure you avoid messy misunderstandings and legal problems. But don't let those requirements intimidate you. The Home School Legal Defense Association (HSLDA) provides parents with free information online outlining each state's requirements. I highly recommend joining the organization, which provides free legal support for members. (The HSLDA has been successfully lobbying education freedom all across the US since 1983.)[60]

The HSLDA also has information in an international section on it's website with the status of homeschooling regulations in countries around the world. You can also find contact information for people involved in homeschooling in each country.

Visit tericapshaw.com/dyingtowin for links and more information.

Homeschool Support Systems

It's difficult to guess exactly how many students are homeschooled in the US. Some studies say as many as two million — more than the number of students attending charter schools.[61] The official number from the Nation Center for Education Statistics (NCES) is just under 1.8 million. Even that number is more than double the number when NCES first started tracking the number of homeschool students in 1999.[62] While that amounts to just 3.4% of the student population, it means it's now easier than ever to find other homeschool families with common interests and goals.

Numerous national, state, and local organizations are available to join. Some are based on specific curriculum with parents organizing to share teaching duties while others focus on field trips, social gatherings, and athletic events. Many homeschool students also benefit from programs open to all youth such as 4-H, Boy Scouts (and other scouting organizations), and athletic organizations. In some states students are allowed to join in extracurricular activities at local public and charter schools. Some private schools also have support programs for homeschool families.

Visit tericapshaw.com/dyingtowin for more information about available options.

Convincing Others

When the quality of our children's education is on the line it is essential to have a solid plan — and it's no wonder family members and friends often seem to reel at the very suggestion of home education. For people who have never seriously considered homeschooling this can sound like some crazy experiment. (I sure thought so when I was five years old. I know, everybody's a skeptic.)

Indeed, your homeschool will only be as good as your family makes it, but these days we aren't just taking a shot in the dark. We now have some data showing the incredible value of parental dedication. In 2007, the HSLDA commissioned Dr. Brian Ray to conduct a study of homeschooling across the United States. He found that homeschooled students tested well above average in all subject areas. In language, math, and science the national average for homeschool students was 84%. They came in at 86% for science and 89% in reading.[63]

But what was most interesting was the negligible impact of family income, gender, amount spent per student, family income, and the parents' educational attainment. In families where both parents graduated from college students did score an average seven points higher (90%) than those in families where neither parent graduated from college. But both groups are far above the national average. The biggest surprise was probably that students with a parent who is a certified teacher only outscored other homeschool students by one percentage point (88% vs. 87%).

An earlier study, also conducted by Ray, addressed the bigger picture: how do homeschooled students fare as adults? His 2003 survey found they were more likely to go on to college than the general population and had greater levels of civic involvement.[64] They were also more likely to report that they were happy with their lives than the general population including job satisfaction, finances, and a general "happiness quotient." Of course, this doesn't mean that homeschooling is a simple formula for a perfect life. Two percent of homeschool alumni reported that they're "not too happy." But when you compare that to 9.4% of the general population it's reasonable to conclude things turned out better for many homeschooled students than naysayers could have fathomed years ago.

Probably the most telling part of the survey has to do with how those homeschooled students looked back on their experience as adults. Most were "glad that I was homeschooled as a student." Of course, not everyone was onboard: 1.4% disagreed with that statement while 0.6% marked "strongly disagree" on their surveys. Seventy-four percent went on to homeschool their own children.

(You can read all the details about these studies online. Just head over to tericapshaw.com/dyingtowin for more information.)

Ultimately, the most important factor in your decision-making process should be what's best for your family and the legacy you're creating together. Enjoying time as a family is a big part of what has kept Paul and Tori Fish homeschooling all these years. "You may go into some public space and you'll run across a family who's different — and it's tough in the immediate sense to figure out why they're different but there's something that catches your attention." Paul says, "And nine times out of ten I've found that you look and you realize 'Oh, actually the family is all together.' Whether that's a parent with two children or whether that's parents with a lot of children. They're all together and they actually enjoy being together. And that's a rare thing to find in this day and age."

Paul says he believes that homeschooling fosters that attitude, "In fact you need to have that if you're going to have a fun time while you're homeschooling — it has very little to do with academics, but when people see that they're immediately attracted to it."

PROFILE
Will Estrada: Defending Parents' Right to Educate

William Estrada describes the opportunity to work for the Homeschool Legal Defense Association (HSLDA) as a dream job he's enjoyed working at for more than 12 years.

As an attorney and Director of Federal Relations for HSLDA, he not only understands the legal arguments in favor of homeschooling — he also understands the deep personal reasons many families have for choosing to homeschool. After all, he was educated at home himself.

Will's parents certainly had a solid understanding of education. His father spent 37 years as a State of New York special education teacher working with high school students. Even in retirement he continues to work as a substitute teacher. Will's mother also worked as a teacher in Boston when she first graduated from college.

Despite their backgrounds as public school educators, Will says a few months after he was born his parents became Christians and soon realized that they didn't want their children in the secular public school environment of upstate New York.

The couple decided to look at private Christian schools, but that simply wasn't affordable on a public school teacher's income. Then they started hearing about a new concept: homeschooling. Will says they decided to try it and it was a hit with the whole family, "They loved it, we loved it as kids, and they kind of never looked back."

Will says religious reasons motivated his parents to homeschool him and his seven younger siblings, but other considerations only reinforced their commitment. As educators, they witnessed the problems common inside school walls — from bullying to the influence of illegal drugs. They were convinced they could do a better job educating their kids at home without those distractions.

Will says choosing to defend parents' right to homeschool their kids wasn't an obvious career choice early on, "When you're 10-years-old and struggling with your math homework and not understanding what you're trying to do you're not thinking 'I want to go and defend homeschool freedom!'"

But during his high school years he started reading the *HSLDA Court Report* publication. He says, "Seeing that kind of battle for freedom, the freedom fighters of the HSLDA lawyers, I said, 'Whoa, that would be cool to work there.'"

He loved literature, reading, and the law and already knew he wanted to become a lawyer. He started off as a legal assistant at HSLDA as he finished law school and continued working with the organization after graduating.

Will says homeschooling, "worked out perfectly" for his parents, yet he doesn't discount the immense pressure every parent faces in deciding what's best for their kids. "No matter how prepared a parent is you always wonder 'Am I going to give my child the best education they can receive? Are they going to get all those good experiences that will prepare them for college? Can I do it?' I know every parent worries about that."

Now with young sons of his own, Will says, "You know your own failings as a parent and things that you wish you could do better." And so, like all parents who spend years doing their best — and want only the best for their children — he says his parents were relieved to see their children successful as adults. And they can rest assured that they not only gave their oldest son a great education, but also sparked in him a desire to make sure as many families as possible have the same opportunities in the future.

Will and his wife Rachel (who is also a homeschool graduate) live in northern Virginia with their two young sons.

GROWING AS A FAMILY

Actress, author, and international model Sam Sorbo has written a book I love to share with others about her "journey from self-doubter to home school advocate."[7] The first half of *They're YOUR Kids* provides fascinating insights into troubling changes in the United States' public education system over time. The second half details her own homeschool approach with her three children.[65] Her second book helps families focus on what matters most: character development. *Teach from Love: A School Year Devotional for Families* provides brief, but deep, daily Bible study plans designed to teach simple lessons and prompt important conversations.[66] Visit www.tericapshaw. com/dyingtowin for more information.

CHAPTER REVIEW

Studies show parental dedication pays off with most homeschool students thriving academically — and leading fulfilling lives as adults.

Nature Walks and Latin Roots

"Get 'shining eyes' first, and the coveted question,
'Can't you read more?' will come."

Susan Schaeffer Macaulay
When Children Love to Learn

Truly great homeschooling, as an extension of great parenting, requires an incredible amount of dedication to doing what's best for each unique child. First, you have to care deeply about every little detail of your child's education. Then you have to care enough to step back and let your child do exactly what he or she was made to do: absorb the wonders of this world we live in.

I find some of the most beautiful concepts for what education is — and should be — at an intersection between teaching methods developed by the late British educator Charlotte Mason and classical education.

There are many interpretations of these two methods — and I don't follow either strictly — but the essence of each can teach us two things.

1) Your child may be capable of far more than you imagine.

2) Your child's abilities will unfold over time — trying to rush the process won't help.

Charlotte Mason Approach

Charlotte Mason founded the Parent's National Education Union (P.N.E.U.) in 1887 and a teacher training college five years later. The motto for the P.N.E.U. was, "Education is an atmosphere, a discipline, and a life."[67]

She did not believe in isolating children in a "child-environment" as she said it, "stultifies a child to bring down his world to the child's level." Instead, she wanted parents and teachers to recognize the educational value of the child's natural home environment and "let him live freely among his proper conditions."

Charlotte Mason's emphasis on discipline referred to the creation of habits of mind and body, "formed definitely and thoughtfully."

She also emphasized the importance of sustaining a child's physical, moral, and intellectual life — arguing that children are also born with a natural appetite to feed their minds as well as their bodies. She wrote that in the approach in P.N.E.U. schools was to give a student, "a full and generous curriculum; taking care only that all knowledge offered to him is vital, that is, that facts are not presented without their informing ideas."

In creating a syllabus for a normal child, she considered three points:

"(A) He requires *much* knowledge, for the mind needs sufficient food as much as does the body.

(B) The knowledge should be various for sameness in mental diet does not create appetite (*i.e.* curiosity)

(C) Knowledge should be communicated in well-chosen language, because his attention responds naturally to what is conveyed in literary form."

She also wrote that, "knowledge is not assimilated until it is reproduced." So, students were called on to "tell-back" what they remembered from a single reading of a book, commonly called "narration."

Although simple, these principles are timeless. A school day that includes reading from "living books", "map work", crafts, and nature walks can provide students with a strong desire to learn, and retain, an amazing amount of important information about the world.

Sonlight is one company providing curriculum loaded with fascinating books to help parents take a Charlotte Mason approach — and my husband and I often find ourselves every bit as interested in the stories as our kids.

Some excellent textbooks can also bring learning to life. My children and I love Apologia's science textbooks which take an "immersion approach." That means that rather than providing only a survey of "grade appropriate" information each book takes a deep dive into a specific area of study. The material is fascinating for the entire family and provides satisfactory answers to so many questions buzzing around in little heads.

For more information and resources inspired by Charlotte Mason visit www.tericapshaw.com/dyingtowin.

Classical Education

My daughter loves to study Latin. That's right, Latin. She seems to be one of those kids who want to dive deep into their work. For certain kids this rigorous approach to learning is both challenging and fun. And it's never been easier to get high quality classical curriculum.

In an era where educational standards are regularly called into question, parents are increasingly turning to this time-tested method based on three stages of learning: the grammar stage, the logic stage, and the rhetoric stage.

It's based on the idea that young students in the grammar stage are developmentally ready to memorize all kinds of information about the world. Students in the middle grades are in the logic stage — ready to analyze and form intelligent arguments. The next stage, rhetoric, is where older students learn to take what they've learned from the earlier stages and form persuasive arguments.

Numerous private schools, charter schools, homeschool co-ops, and homeschool curriculums now offer classical education programs.

The Highlands Latin School in Louisville, Kentucky is one school taking a classical Christian approach — and achieving phenomenal results. The school has an enrollment of 627 students with an average 16 students per classroom.

The school's three-year SAT score average is 1372 and the ACT score average is 30. In 2015 the school's students scored in the top one-percent of all schools in the nation on the Iowa Test of Basic Skills (ITBS) — for the 12th year in a row.[68]

That means Highlands Latin School Kindergarteners are performing as well as average second graders while their second graders are performing as well as the average fourth grader. By fourth grade, their students are working at a seventh-grade level and by sixth grade, they are testing as well as the average high school sophomore. By seventh grade, the Highlands Latin School students receive the maximum possible grade equivalency on the ITBS: "13+."

As a result, graduates from this little school in Kentucky have been accepted at some of the most prestigious colleges in the world including MIT. And they're apparently doing that in far fewer school hours than Asian students competing for entrance at some of the same prestigious colleges.

Kindergarteners at Highlands Latin School spend just two days in class while those in the next two grades have a three-day week. Students in grades 3-12 step up to a four-day week — although the students are still expected to spend one day each week on homework.

Since the school also produces homeschool curriculum through Memoria Press, I have a bit of insight into how they're experiencing so much success using an old education model with modern kids.

Their curriculum for young students includes elements as serious as studying Latin starting in the second grade and yet also incorporates colorful, bright books including titles from the Cat in The Hat Learning Library for science. The result is age appropriate challenging work that takes kids seriously and yet still allows them to enjoy just being kids.

Visit tericapshaw.com/dyingtowin for more information about classical education and a sample of all the great resources available.

A Mother's Wisdom

In her book, *Mere Motherhood*, Cindy Rollins teaches, entertains, and prompts her readers to think deeply. Through the book, she tells the story of meeting and marrying her husband, then homeschooling the eight sons and one daughter who came along as the years passed. At times lighthearted, the book also includes sharp doses of reality for the benefit of her readers as she looks at homeschooling and young motherhood in hindsight.

Imperfect Life, Great Education

If you feel like you don't have the "perfect" family required for homeschooling or even to support your kids in their work at school — welcome to the club! We *all* fall short of our ideal. When reality crashes in and seems to defeat your dreams it can be demoralizing, but our kids can grow stronger as they see how we deal with struggles. For single parents, the job will be much more difficult, but you can still have a huge positive impact. My mom did and some of my friends are still going through that process.

Some families have also experienced horrific life events that make homeschooling seem almost impossible in light of the hardship. The Home School Foundation is a charitable arm of HSLDA providing grants to widows, single parents, children with special needs, military families, low-income families, and those needing help following a natural disaster.[69]

Families can apply online for help. You can also find information to donate and volunteer to the organization. Visit tericapshaw.com/dyingtowin for a link.

CHAPTER REVIEW

Your children are likely capable of far more than you can even imagine. A good approach and quality curriculum can help cultivate and feed their appetites for learning.

INSIDE OUR HOMESCHOOL

"The worst attitude of all would be the professional attitude which regards children in the lump as a sort of raw material which we have to handle. We must, of course, try to do them no harm. We may under the omnipotence sometimes dare to hope that we may do them good, but only such good that involves treating them with respect. We must not imagine that we are providence or destiny.

C.S. Lewis
The Art of Writing & The Gifts of Writers

Sweat was streaming down his face as my two-year-old struggled up a hill past slides in Tiger Mountain Park in Taoyuan. At one point the *Usborne Children's Dictionary* slipped away from him and tumbled downhill, but he managed to keep a firm grip on *Living Long Ago*.

With a bit of help, he finally made it to a cement ledge where he sat down to study in earnest. Soon he had the attention of several grandmas asking me a dozen questions in Chinese and trying to convince their little ones (who were generally appalled by the idea) that they should sit down and join him. Times like this — when my baby gleefully shows me that he can find the "Roman times" all by himself — show me that we have tapped into the magic homeschooling has to offer.

Places Where We Study

At this moment in time our house, or rather, apartment, is equipped with a schoolroom/playroom. It's perhaps telling that the best feature is a fully padded floor. (We do have four children age seven and under.)

It's nice to have child-sized desks and chairs for handwriting, so the child is in the correct position. However, for other subjects, we study in any location that's convenient. Around the house that's most likely where there's a pile of laundry that Mom needs to fold.

But the best learning happens on days when we can spend a lot of time outside. The kids run and play then settle down for a story in the shade. Sometimes my oldest daughter will answer a workbook problem or recitation question every time she runs a lap around the playground. My oldest son will run up and read an *All About Reading* word card then run off and play some more.

This is not only more fun that sitting at a table, but it makes a lot of sense for young kids who need plenty of physical activity to help complete lower brain development. The more my kids get the physical exercise they need the easier it is to get them to settle down and focus when appropriate.

We also take advantage of time spent in the car by playing great audio books such as the *Story of the World* history books by Susan Wise Bauer or good quality children's literature available through Audible (periodically available at greatly reduced prices). Sometimes we put on the audio version of an Apologia textbook while the kids color in their Junior Notebooking Journals.

We also use music CDs to help kids memorize anything from Bible verses to geography facts. It's also an opportunity to get foreign language practice in by playing our Rocket

Chinese lessons from an app on my smartphone. (Something we apparently need to do more often. In the words of my four-year-old son, "Hey, if we keep listening to this stuff I might start to know what's going on when people in Taiwan are talking at me.")

When We Study

At this point, we have a very casual year-round school schedule which I map out on an Excel sheet. I love being at a place where we're a bit ahead of what is expected for the kids' ages so there's never any question as to whether we're getting enough done.

However, since it isn't required by law, I don't worry about meeting every educational standard — especially not in the specific order listed. Nothing increases my compassion and respect for public school teachers like reading educational standards. (I'd like to see a reality show where average people try to take over a kindergarten class.) Making my kids cover extremely detailed checklists isn't necessary when my kids are learning naturally. Instead of teaching to a list of standards specifically, I monitor the children's development to make sure there are no gaps developing without a specific plan to address them.

I make sure we're reading plenty of high quality books, placing an emphasis on phonics and reading instruction, and creating a solid foundation for math skills. I want to ensure we have kids well equipped for lifelong learning.

Of course, just as schools have specific standards to meet for a reason, I do periodically evaluate how the kids are doing and identify weak points we need to work on. This might include anything from handwriting to social skills. (I'm looking at you warrior-boy.) It's amazing the difference intense focus on a certain area will make. For instance, when my daughter was far ahead in every area except handwriting, I made 10 minutes of handwriting practice the first thing she tackled every day for a few months. Since she didn't really like to do it, I didn't make her write at any other time during the day. Before long she was at grade level in that area.

I also make sure to watch for warning signs that something is off. For instance I make sure to get eye examinations to ensure they will be able to read clearly. Since my children were all born with upper lip ties I checked with a specialist to see if one child in particular would need speech therapy. This book doesn't specifically address developmental problems, but many of my friend have experienced issues their children needed help with. Young children tend to hit certain developmental milestones at different times, but if it seems like something is off I strongly suggest looking into any possible problems. It's good to get therapy to help correct problems early on.

Most of the time, we start subjects requiring the most effort from the kids in the morning when they're still feeling sharp (never mind that mom is still painfully groggy). Read aloud books are perfect for afternoons when the kids are ready to just listen and let their imaginations get lost in the story. For some reason, non-fiction reference books tend to be most popular when they are ready for a break from physical play. Of course, I read them whenever I deem appropriate, but I have noticed that the drier material seems to come alive when they're ready to take a break at a playground or park.

How We Study

When people see my now seven-year-old daughter pick up *The Blue Fairy Book* (Lexile Reading Level of average 10th graders) and read it almost flawlessly, they are generally surprised.

They would be stunned if they could see back in time. I still don't know how that girl ever learned to read. We only studied phonics for 15 minutes a day — and it seems that she spent half of our lessons staring at the ceiling and the other half morphing into a floppy mass that would slip off my lap and under the rocking chair.

My focus is not on how the learning process looks, but rather on making genuine connections with the child and providing exactly what he or she needs to be challenged, surprised, and delighted in turn. I couldn't care less whether it *looks* like the kids are learning. Results alone are what matters. Of course, they also need to learn appropriate behavior. But I'm careful not to bundle behavior problems with unrelated academic challenges.

We read aloud a lot. We regularly tackle challenging math problems with manipulatives, worksheets, and computer programs. We recite information to memorize and, on rare occasions, complete workbooks.

We discuss deep theology topics regularly because my kids get a mischievous joy out of testing mom. I'm convinced intense conversations now will lay a foundation for the teen years 10 years from now. We also spend hours playing videos: Curious George, The Cat in the Hat Knows a Lot About That, LeapFrog, PureFlix homeschool video recommendations, and anything on Jelly Telly. Sometimes we watch National Geographic videos — even though that sales guy totally lied about the "no-blood" part.

We talk a lot about who we are and the people who make up our world — past and present. Perhaps, the most important thing about successful homeschooling is that it's not really all about home, but about building a strong foundation that prepares us for the contributions we can make — and the lessons we can learn — when we venture out into this big wonderful world.

AFTERWORD

Wow. If you're like me — with a baby tugging on one leg and a toddler patting a sticky hand on your opposite arm — getting all the way through this book has likely been quite the journey. Or maybe you're at a cleaner stage of parenting, but facing weightier questions concerning how you will direct these increasingly independent and competent young people. Or maybe you're reading through the wisdom found only in parenting hindsight. Perhaps you're contemplating what the future holds when you become a parent. In any case, I thank you for the gift of your time.

More than anything I hope this has read as a love story. I hope it has encouraged you to hold your children closer in the appropriate season and yet step back and give them opportunities to strengthen their wings so they can learn to fly.

My inspiration for this book was seeing my pre-school aged daughter grow into second grade work by the time she was old enough to go to kindergarten. It was work she did in the time many of her peers spent reluctantly doing "pre-school homework" — and it was deep work she truly loved with the satisfaction of an athlete who has trained to run a race well.

I hope the stories within this book have given you a vision — not to use our children to vicariously achieve greatness — but to give ordinary children extraordinary freedom to learn.

Finally, I haven't alluded to my Christian faith much in this book as it didn't factor largely in the questions at hand, but rather, I hope, serves as a foundation for all I do.

Early on in this project a mother wiser than myself, Pat Broomfield Bradley, shared her prayer for this book.

"He told me to tell you to pray for His wisdom to instruct you and guide you in the way you should go and the decisions you should make that you are not to lean only on your understanding nor the understanding of your critics. You are to trust Him, the Lord, acknowledge Him in all your ways. Trust that he will direct you in the path you should go."

This sentiment from the Book of Proverbs sums up my aspirations for how I will journey through life as a mother, teacher, writer, wife, and child of God. I desire the wisdom to discern the way I should go. I thank you for joining me for this short portion of the journey and hope is has provided some nourishing food for thought as you chart your own course.

Notes

1. Amanda Little, Bloomberg Businessweek, "Fixing the Best Schools in the World", September 25, 2014, https://www.bloomberg.com/news/articles/2014-09-24/chinas-education-reform-push-extends-to-shanghais-top-schools.

2. Amy Tan, "Girl's suicide highlights the stress children face in Singapore", Reuters News Service, New Straits Times, August 29, 2001.

3. Chang Shook and Cheong Agnes, "Implementation of the 'Thinking Schools, Learning Nation' Initiative in Singapore", Journal of Southeast Asian Education 2001, Vol. 2, No. 1, pp. 13-41.

4. Shirley Zhao, "The Shocking Rise of Child Suicide", December 7, 2011, timeout.com/hong-kong.

5. "What's Wrong with Chinese Children: 500 School Students Commit Suicide Each Year in China", May 16, 2014, ntd.tv.

6. Tom Phillips, "Chinese School Installs 'Anti-Suicide' Barriers Before Dreaded Exam", April 21, 2015, The Telegraph.

7. Hou Liqicang and Zhang Yu, "Tough regime cranks out test winners", June 6, 2014, http://www.chinadaily.com.cn/2014-06/06/content_17566975.htm.

8. Rachel Lu, "China's Cram School from Hell", October 11, 2013, http://foreignpolicy.com/2013/10/11/chinas-cram-school-from-hell/.

9. Valerie Strauss, "Chinese Students Use IV Amino Acids to Study for High-Stakes Tests", May 10, 2012, The Washington Post.

10. OECD (2014), *PISA 2012 Results in Focus: What 15-year-olds know and what they can do with what they know*, (OECD Publishing), https://www.oecd.org/pisa/keyfindings/pisa-2012-results-overview.pdf.

11. Shirley S. Wang, "The Puzzling Rise in Nearsighted Children", April 20, 2015, The Wall Street Journal.

12. Shelley Rigger, *Why Taiwan Matters: Small Island, Global Powerhouse*, (Rowman & Littlefield Publishers, Inc., 2011).

13. Common Core Standards Initiative Myths vs. Facts, October 21, 2015, http://www.corestandards.org/about-the-standards/myths-vs-facts/

14. OECD (2013), *Lessons from PISA 2012 for the United States, Strong Performers and Successful Reformers in Education*, (OECD Publishing), http://dx.doi.org10.1787/9789264207585-en.

15. Benjamin Hansen and Matthew Lang, "Back to School Blues: Seasonality of youth suicide and the academic calendar", Economics of Education Review 30, 2011, 850-861.

16. David Elkind, Ph.D., *The Hurried Child: Growing Up Too Fast Too Soon*, Third Edition, (Da Capo Press, 2007).

17. Building the Machine, Ian Reid, (HSLDA, 2014).

18. Amanda Ripley, "The $4 Million Teacher", The Wall Street Journal, August 3, 2013, http://www.wsj.com/articles/SB10001424127887324635904578639780253571520.

19. James Marshall Crotty, "Global Private Tutoring Market Will Surpass 102.8 Billion by 2018", Forbes, October 30, 2012.

20. "Online Education Market in China", EUSME Centre, October 7, 2014.

21. Josh Chin, "Value of a Chinese Degree: $44?", Wall Street Journal, November 22, 2010.

22. Chuing Prudence Chou, "Education in Taiwan: Taiwan's Colleges and Universities", Brookings, November 2014.

23. Wu Hui-lin, "Depreciating value of education", Taipei Times, May 29, 2013.

24. Valerie Strauss, "And now… Common Core tutors", Washington Post, November 26, 2013.

25. "Education at a Glance", OECD, 2011.

26. Lawrence Delevingne, "Companies cash in on Common Core despite controversy", CNBC, March 11, 2015.

27. Rachel Rooney and Evan White, "Students begin Saturday classes in New Haven", Eyewitness News 3, January 9, 2016, http://www.wfsb.com/story/30924458/students-begin-saturday-classes-in-new-haven#ixzz3xle30ZlF

28. Jason Whitely and WFAA, "Restoring recess: Why Dallas ISD wants to make it mandatory again", WFAA 8 ABC, January 19, 2016, http://www.wfaa.com/story/news/education/2016/01/19/restoring-recess-why-dallas-isd-wants-make-mandatory-again/79040468/.

29. Lyndsey Layton, "Study says standardized testing is overwhelming nation's public schools", The Washington Post, October 24, 2015, https://www.washingtonpost.com/local/education/study-says-standardized-testing-is-overwhelming-nations-public-schools/2015/10/24/8a22092c-79ae-11e5-a958-d889faf561dc_story.html?utm_term=.a57cfdca2679.

30. David and Micki Colfax, Homeschooling for Excellence, (Warner Books edition; First eBook Edition, April 2009).

31. Ken Robinson (2006), Do Schools Kill Creativity? [Video file], https://www.ted.com/talks/ken_robinson_says_schools_kill_creativity/transcript.

32. Joseph Murphy, Homeschooling in America, (Corwin, 2012).

33. David and Micki Colfax, Hard Times in Paradise, (Warner Books, 1992).

34. EdX, August 23, 2017, https://www.edx.org/.

35. Tsh Oxenreider, "Organized Simplicity: The Clutter-Free Approach to Intentional Living", Betterway Home Books, 2010.

36. Tom Jacobs, "The Value of Unstructured Play Time for Kids", Pacific Standard, May 9, 2014.

37. "The Joys of Doing Nothing", Scholastic.com, printed from website November 6, 2015.

38. Sarah Mackenzie, *Teaching From Rest: A Homeschooler's Guide to Unshakable Peace*, (Classical Academic Press, 2015).

39. Amy McCready, *If I Have to Tell You One More TIME…: The Revolutionary Program That Gets Your Kids to Listen Without Nagging, Reminding, or Yelling*, (Penguin Group, 2011).

40. Sarah Lybrand, "From bullied to bank: How Bethany Mota created a YouTube and fashion empire, Yahoo Finance, April 21, 2014, https://finance.yahoo.com/blogs/driven/bullied-to-bank —bethany-mota-s-youtube-empire-133655143.html

41. Proverbs 20:5, *Holy Bible: New American Standard Bible*. 1995. LaHabra, CA: The Lockman Foundation. As found in the YouVersion Bible App.

42. Kelly Day, "11 Ways Finland's Education System Shows Us that 'Less is More', fillingmymap.com, April 15, 2015, https://fillingmymap.com/2015/04/15/11-ways-finlands-education-system-shows-us-that-less-is-more/

43. John Maxwell, *Intentional Living*, (Center Street 2015).

44. Timothy A. Pychyl, "Education Is Not the Filling of a Pail, But the Lighting of a Fire", May 10, 2008, https://www.psychologytoday.com/blog/dont-delay/200805/education-is-not-the-filling-pail-the-lighting-fire.

45. Kathy H. Lee and Lesli M. Richards, *A Year of Playing Skillfully*, (The Homegrown Preschooler, 2014).

46. Bob Tebow Evangelistic Association, "Tebow Family", http://www.btea.org/aboutus.asp.

47. "Tebow Bills Gain Ground on Equality for Homeschoolers", July 2, 2013, https://www.aop.com/blog/tebow-bills-gain-ground-on-equality-for-homeschoolers.

48. Crystal Paine, "A Dream Come True: Paying Cash for Our First Home", July 8, 2010, http://moneysavingmom.com/series/saving-100-down-for-a-home.

49. Moneysavingmom.com, "About Me", http://moneysavingmom.com/about

50. Joyce Swann, *Looking Backward: My Twenty-Five Years as a Homeschooling Mother*, (Frontier 2000 Media Group, 2010).

51. Grace Bush: http://www.today.com/news/not-hard-just-hard-work-girl-16-graduates-high-school-2D79637124

52. Kip and Mona Lisa Harding, *The Brainy Bunch: The Harding Family's Method to College Ready by Age 12*, (Gallery Books, 2014).

53. Ellie Zolfagharifard, "Elon Musk create the world's most exclusive school: Entrepreneur reveals he bought a mansion to house 20 pupils (including his five kids) and three teachers, September 24, 2015, http://www.dailymail.co.uk/sciencetech/article-3247968/Elon-Musk-creates-world-s-exclusive-school-Entrepreneur-reveals-bought-mansion-house-15-pupils-including-five-kids-three-teachers.html.

54. Kwame Opam, "Elon Musk created his own grade school for the children of SpaceX employees", May 22, 2015, https://www.theverge.com/2015/5/22/8646683/elon-musk-school-spacex-children

55. "Prepare for MIT", printed August 24, 2015, http://mitadmissions.org/apply/prepare/homeschool.

56. Mark LaMaster, *Friday Nigh Lights for Fathers and Sons: Schedule a 10-game winning season to help develop your son into the man God intended him to be, (Author Academy Elite 2015).*

57. Cindy Rollins, *Mere Motherhood*, (CIRCE Institute 2016).

58. Adventure Nannies, "Private Educators", https://www. adventurenannies.com/services/private-educators/

59. Trivium Pursuit Blog, "Homeschooling in Iowa in the 1970s", http://www.triviumpursuit.com/blog/2006/04/03/ homeschooling-in-iowa-in-the-1970s/.

60. Home School Legal Defense Association, https://www.hslda. org/laws/default.asp.

61. Joseph Murphy, *Homeschooling in America*, (Corwin, 2012).

62. J. Michael Smith, Esq., "U.S. Department of Education: Homeschooling Continues to Grow!", September 3, 2013, https://www.hslda.org/docs/news/2013/201309030.asp.

63. Homeschool Legal Defense Association, "Homeschool Progress Report 2009", https://www.hslda.org/docs/study/ ray2009/2009_Ray_StudyFINAL.pdf.

64. Homeschool Legal Defense Association, "Homeschooling Grows Up", https://www.hslda.org/research/ray2003/.

65. Sam Sorbo, *They're YOUR Kids: An Inspirational Journey from Self-Doubter to Home School Advocate*, (Reveille Press, 2016).

66. Sam Sorbo, *Teach from Love: A School Year Devotional for Families*, (BroadStreet Publishing 2017).

67. Charlotte Mason, *Charlotte Mason's Original Homes Schooling Series*, (Amazon Kindle Edition 2013).

68. Highlands Latin School, "SAT and ITBS Scores", https:// thelatinschool.org/aboutus/satitbsscores/.

69. Homeschool Foundation, "Disaster Relief", https://www. homeschoolfoundation.org/index.php?id=3.

Ready to find irresistible books?

Sign up for a free guide to choosing inspiring curriculum, fun games, and my family's absolute favorite books:
tericapshaw.com

73402789R00097

Made in the USA
Middletown, DE
13 May 2018